**Conversations with Newcastle
players down the decades**

MORE MAGPIE MEMORIES

by Malcolm Holt

breedon **books**
PUBLISHING

First published in Great Britain in 2005 by
The Breedon Books Publishing Company Limited
Breedon House, 3 The Parker Centre,
Derby, DE21 4SZ.

ISBN 1 85983 421 3

Printed and bound by Biddles Ltd, King's Lynn, Norfolk.

Contents

Picture Credits

Introduction

PRE-MATCH NERVES

THE INFAMOUS football match played at St James' Park on 25 August 1999 is likely to haunt Newcastle United supporters for eternity. Ruud Gullit, manager at the time, foolishly chose to bench captain Alan Shearer and the arch enemy Sunderland went on to win the game 2–1 in the worst downpour ever imaginable. This horror show sounded the managerial death knell for Ruud Gullit as his reign ended in the rain and we witnessed the demise of his so-called 'sexy football'.

In stark contrast, the resounding 8–0 thrashing of Sheffield Wednesday at St James' Park on 19 September 1999, in somewhat more hospitable and drier conditions, heralded the arrival of Sir Bobby Robson to the manager's seat at Newcastle United Football Club. The autumn of 1999 brought significant changes for Newcastle United and one particularly seminal experience for me personally.

It was a mere two months after Bobby Robson's first game in charge of Newcastle United that I had my first personal close encounter with country music star turned crime fiction writer turned possible future Governor of Texas, Kinky Friedman. The author of several mystery novels and former columnist for *Texas Monthly* magazine, he now lives with his dogs, pet armadillo, many imaginary horses and a well-used Smith-Corona typewriter in a little green trailer on a ranch in the Texas Hill Country. During that first encounter with Kinky Friedman in his dressing room at the Live Theatre in Newcastle upon Tyne, I asked him if he had a favourite book from his own publications. He fired up a rather large Cuban cigar, blew the smoke past the brim of his equally large black cowboy hat towards the ceiling, and smiled. He answered, 'Oh yeah, that's easy – the next one'.

After completing my first book, *Magpie Memories*, in 2004 and seeing it displayed in the bookshops of Tyneside, I reflected upon that particular encounter some five years earlier. Kinky Friedman's novels contain fictional characters who are actually based on real people in his life. Of course, the people featured in my first book were real people and during their football careers they were real characters. Writing a book and seeing it published inevitably gives you a lot of personal satisfaction. However, although there is very much a sense of 'job done', there is also a strong element of 'what next?'

Magpie Memories was for me a natural progression from the articles that I had penned for the Newcastle United supporters' fanzine *The Mag* over a number of seasons. It proved to be an enlightening journey through time, trawling the development of Newcastle United Football Club over a period of 50 years. The players who I interviewed were all proud to have worn the famous black and white shirt and in their own way, they contributed to the club's history. Before I embarked on this, my second journey through time with Newcastle United, the question that I was frequently asked was, 'What are you going to do now?' Echoing my literary associate from the Lone Star State, I always seemed to reply, 'Oh that's easy, the next one'.

Some time ago, I was reminded of the fact that Agatha Christie wrote *Death on the Nile* while sitting on her verandah at The Old Cataract Hotel in Aswan, Egypt, during a three-month stay. She also used an old typewriter. I embarked on writing *More Magpie Memories* after travelling to Portugal on a football-free weekend in February. FA Cup replays had resulted in the postponement of Newcastle United's away game at Fulham. My lads were on a school holiday for the week, so we left the pedigree mongrel dog in charge of the house, we left Granny in charge of the pedigree mongrel dog and we flew to the Algarve.

The Algarve's name comes from 'Al Garb', which means 'the west', and many of the region's towns have names that begin with 'al'. So it was rather fitting that as we sat in the Coyote Karaoke Bar in Albufeira watching Newcastle United play Heerenveen in Holland in the UEFA Cup, courtesy of a large screen, our own 'Al', Alan Shearer, scored our first goal. It was a really strange game, with some of the travelling supporters chanting 'sack the board' and Lee Bowyer being sent off after scoring the winning goal. However, the game was not as strange as the one at home a month or so later against Aston Villa, during which Lee Bowyer and Kieron Dyer were sent off for fighting each other. At the time I was reminded of an old saying that seemed to be somewhat appropriate to the occasion. 'Whenever you point the finger of blame at somebody else, just remember that there are three fingers pointing back at you.'

As I walked back to our Algarve apartment with the lads after a satisfactory 2–1 first-leg away victory, my mind drifted back to my own teenage years. It may have been a touch of nostalgia, but more likely to have been due to the copious amount of very cheap beer on offer. When I was a young teenager, I used to queue up at the turnstiles along with my friends, waiting to hand over my well-earned pocket money so that I could watch football matches, many of which I can still remember today. Of course, the world of football has changed a lot since those days. In fact, the world has changed. There is now a Starbucks in Jesmond. The game of football has changed, the people have changed and I have changed. I am now several pounds heavier, have a shiny head and sport a beard – not a particularly common sight when I was at school.

If you have ever visited Sea World at Orlando in Florida, you may be familiar with the warning on the back of the car park ticket. For those of you who are unfamiliar with the warning it says, 'Weapons, knives, any other type of sharp objects, straws, coolers and any hazardous items or materials are not permitted in the park'. The same rules apply at our football grounds today. When I was in my youth, you could take anything through the turnstiles – wooden rattles, banners and flags on large poles, even parents, they were all permitted in the ground. I cannot remember ever being frisked for a concealed straw. What is it about these weapons of mass destruction that creates so much fear? Nowadays you could be sprayed with hot Bovril, pelted with rock-hard pies or poked in the eye with an autograph hunter's biro. At least you will be safe in the knowledge that no one can assault you with a straw. Indeed the world of football has changed.

I have to admit that I paid out a lot of well-earned pocket money over the years to watch a great variety of footballers. Some of them could not tackle a Sunday dinner, some could not pass water and some could not hit the proverbial barn door from six inches. Equally I have witnessed performances by some players who were pure geniuses, possessing great skills and even greater personalities. *More Magpie Memories* is another collection of personal interviews with former Newcastle United players, again spanning 50 years. They, whoever 'they' happen to be, said it could not be done the first time and they were even more adamant that it could not be done a second time. Well I was never one to shirk a tackle. I have to confess that I did have some reservations about trying to equal my first performance, but I need not have worried at all. The players in my second line-up were just as willing to recall their memories and their stories are just as unique as those in my first line-up.

There will inevitably be many younger supporters of Newcastle United who were not even born when some of the former players featured in this book graced the pitch at St James' Park. You cannot choose your parents and you cannot influence when you are born. Just ask my pedigree mongrel dog, former resident of the Newcastle Dog and Cat Shelter. She would tell you if she could, 'It is not your fault'. Newcastle United supporters of today, of whatever age, will have ancestors who sat or stood in the same stadium and cheered on the team of their particular era with the same fervour and passion. It is in the blood – you inherit it. A true football supporter is blessed with the essential DNA. True faith is something that you have within you – you cannot buy it.

I remember the occasion when I was sitting in the McDonald's in Northumberland Street in Newcastle and a seven-year-old boy and his father were seated at a nearby table. The boy was wearing an over-sized replica shirt which featured red and white stripes. As the boy tucked into his Happy Meal, I heard him say to his father, 'Dad, when I grow up, I'm going to play for Sunderland'. As I was getting up to leave, having polished off my Big Mac, I leaned over to the father and said, 'Don't worry, he can't do both'.

I have to confess that when I was tapping away on my keyboard, putting this book into some form of logical order, I could often hear the voices of the former players inside my head. It was a little unsettling at first, but I soon came to realise that this was a kind of spiritual connection, another piece of history in the making. It was only when I started to laugh out loud that my curious faithful dog got up and left the room. And so it is with the greatest of pleasure that I am able to announce the following line-up in *More Magpie Memories*:

Ken Prior had two spells with Newcastle United, during 1952–54 and 1956–57. Playing at outside-left, Ken was a talented young footballer who found his career largely frustrated by the ever-presence of Bobby Mitchell in the first team. However, he was still a prolific performer for the reserves at St James' Park.

Dave Hollins, goalkeeper during the period 1961–67, spectacularly saved a penalty during his away debut and then conceded six goals in his first home game. Dave was an agile 'keeper who went on to play for his country.

Keith Kettleborough played in midfield during 1966. Also a keen cricketer, Keith proved to be a shrewd purchase at the time, with Newcastle United struggling to avoid the relegation zone in the old First Division. Keith's command of the midfield proved to be instrumental in turning round the club's fortunes and helped to avoid the drop.

Jim Scott played in midfield and at outside-right during the period 1967–70. Signed from Hibernian, Jim played a prominent role during the successful Inter Cities Fairs Cup campaign in 1969, scoring Newcastle United's first-ever European goal. He also netted crucial goals in the semi-final and the final.

Irving Nattrass played right-back during the period 1970–79. A graduate of the junior structure at St James' Park, he was an assured performer who ultimately captained Newcastle United. Unfortunately for Irving, injuries were to disrupt his overall progress and they sadly prevented him from pursuing what would likely have been a successful international career.

Tony Green, a true midfield genius, only played two seasons at St James' Park, during the period 1971–73, before being forced to retire early through injury. Tony became an instant idol on Tyneside and is still highly thought of today. For many supporters of his era, Tony is still regarded as one of the best players ever to wear the black and white shirt.

John Tudor, a striker during the period 1971–76, forged an explosive partnership with Malcolm Macdonald over four seasons, becoming a genuine favourite with the supporters on Tyneside. A couple of years after leaving Newcastle United, John was forced to retire through injury. He subsequently moved to the USA in 1994 and is now a director of football coaching.

Micky Burns, a striker who often played from midfield, was at St James' Park during the period 1974–78. Following the departure of Malcolm Macdonald, Micky was the top goalscorer for two consecutive seasons. He was also one of the players who were at the centre of the so-called 'Players' Revolt'.

Mick Martin played in midfield during the period 1978–83. Known as 'Zico' even today to the Toon Army faithful, Mick gave good service to Newcastle United, returning later to coach and scout for the club. Mick settled in the area and is a pundit for one of the local radio stations.

John Anderson, who arrived on a free transfer from Preston North End, having been released by former Newcastle United manager Gordon Lee, proved himself to be a versatile right-back and centre-half, playing during the period 1982–92. After retiring through injury, John settled in the area and is also now a local radio pundit.

Billy Whitehurst was a centre-forward who played during the period 1985–86. A former bricklayer, miner's son Billy was a big man on the field as well as off it. Billy's footballing style often courted controversy, but he was a true character throughout his career and always gave maximum effort on the field.

Warren Barton played right-back during the period 1995–2002 and when signed he was Britain's most expensive defender. One of Kevin Keegan's 'Entertainers', Warren proved himself to be a great servant to Newcastle United and is always given a warm welcome whenever he is back on Tyneside.

The interviews for this second book were carried out between July 2004 and January 2005 and they enabled me to complete another fascinating journey through time. I have again tried to cover all areas of the football pitch and have again travelled over 50 years. Throughout this second journey I have again welcomed the support of my family and I remain forever grateful to my colleague and fellow Newcastle United supporter Allan Jacques for his constructive comments and personal support.

I am delighted to have had the support of all the team at Breedon Books for a second time and wish to thank them for all their hard work in producing this book. Finally, I am yet again immensely grateful to all the players who were more than willing to give up their valuable time to be interviewed by myself. Without their co-operation this book would not have been possible. These are their special Magpie memories in black and white.

Chapter 1

KEN PRIOR
(1952–54, 1956–57)

KENNETH GEORGE PRIOR was born on 13 October 1932 in Newcastle upon Tyne. Playing as an outside-left for the club, Ken had two spells at St James' Park. He signed professional with the club in March 1952 before being transferred to Millwall in May 1954 for £100. He returned to Newcastle United in July 1956, costing the club £1,250. Ken made 10 senior starts for the club and scored three goals. Although his first-team appearances were limited, Ken regularly played for the reserves and was a well-respected footballer in the North East. Like many from his era, his football career began at school.

'I got into football when I was 12, playing for Bothal School in like the local school league. Then I went from there to the East Northumberland team and then to the Northumberland team. Then after school I played for Cambois Juniors 14–16 team and then the 16–18 team. And Jackie Milburn took us through to Newcastle and I had a trial in the B team. That game was played against Hugh Wood, a mining company team somewhere beside the Team Valley. It was that way somewhere, just beside where their factory was.

'Newcastle kept us on as an amateur and sent for us here and there. Then "Tot" Smith, the centre-half, he started to run the team. I got picked for the A team and was playing there for a season. Then I was training one Thursday night and Stan Seymour waved us into the tunnel and he said, "You're playing against Middlesbrough on Saturday in the derby at St James' Park." So I literally went from the A team to the first team in a week. That was my debut on 11 April 1952 at St James' Park against Middlesbrough. I think there were about 60,000 people there and as we were walking out of the tunnel, Jackie Milburn was walking behind us. He tapped us on the shoulder and he says, "Oh by the way, I forgot to tell you, if we get a penalty kick you're taking it." I nearly died. Never mind, I had a good game according to the paper, like.

'So then I basically played in the reserves after that. Then I turned part-time professional. I was an apprentice electrician, you see, and I wanted to finish my time before I went full-time professional. I was like unsure whether to gan full-time or not. But never mind, the opportunity arose and I'd finished my time and I played for one more season. Then they transferred us to Millwall.

I played at Millwall for two seasons and we were playing at Charlton. I've forgotten what League they were in at the time. I can't remember if it was the reserve team or the floodlight. It was at the old Valley anyway. They had a Floodlight Cup, a London Floodlight Cup, and that was on, so I cannot really remember what game it was. But Sam Bartram was in goal and we beat them 6–1 and I scored four goals. When I came off the pitch, this chap comes up to us and says, "Would you like to gan back to Newcastle?" I says, "Oh, I divvn't know, I'm happy here." He says, "Well, Stan Seymour wants you to gan back." I says, "Stan does?"

'So anyway, I went back to the club. The manager at Millwall called us in and he says, "Would you like to go back to Newcastle, Ken?" I says, "Well, I divvn't know." He says, "I'll be honest with you mind, Bolton Wanderers want you to go there. They've been on the phone." Anyway, I plumped for Newcastle. I think that my wife was expecting her first bairn and she wanted to be home. So I says, "We'll gan back to Newcastle." So I went back to Newcastle and I played in the first team, but I played mostly in the reserves. Then I got injured at Wolverhampton. I twisted my knee and done my knee ligaments. I was out for nine weeks. And I picked the local paper up during this nine weeks stint and it's got written on the back of the paper, "Paterson and Prior up for transfer". I says, "I can't be up for transfer, that must be a misprint. I haven't played for nine weeks." Bill Paterson had taken over from Frank Brennan, and when I went into the ground, he shouted us over. He says, "Have you seen the paper?" I says, "Aye, what's it all about?"

'So, Stan Seymour came out of the tunnel and I went across. I said, "Stan, what's this in the paper?" He says, "Why, you haven't been playing very well, have you, Ken?" I says, "Stan, I haven't played for nine weeks. I've never kicked a ball for nine weeks. I got hurt at Wolverhampton." He says, "Oh why, I've had some funny reports." Not mentioning any names, but I knew who it was, he did the same with Tommy Casey. Stan says, "Will you gan out on loan 'til you get yourself match fit?" I says, "Aye, where?" He says, "What about Berwick?" I says, "Berwick?" He says, "Aye, I'll have a word with Anderson, the chairman." So he had a word with the chairman and I duly ended up there. I says "I'm not going for any less money, mind. I've just been married not so long ago and I'm not going for any less money." I mean, the money was only 18 quid anyway.

'I went to see Anderson, the chairman, and he says, "Okay, we'll just take the contract over." So I played for Berwick. While I was there, Raith Rovers came in for me. Anyway, Newcastle wouldn't let us gan. So I went back to Newcastle during the '56–57 season and I played. I couldn't believe it, they gave us a free transfer at the end of the season. They stopped us gannin' to Raith Rovers so they could give us a free transfer. I'd had a wonderful offer from Raith Rovers. They offered us a free house, £30 a week, and another £30 off the chairman. He was the owner of a furniture factory. He was going to put us on the books and pay us from the factory. But that never materialised. It was a really good offer. So I says to myself, "I'm sick of this".

'Darlington wanted us to gan there, but I said that I wasn't travelling there. So, what I did, I went semi-professional again and I went back to my trade. I went to North Shields and started to play for them. Frank Brennan also went to North Shields. I played for them for a few years, then they turned amateur and I couldn't play. So I went to Horden and then from there I went to Ashington. I played a couple of years there and then I got the player-manager's job and later I got the manager's job. I was there for nine years and then I went to Alnwick. I managed Alnwick for a while, but in between all of that I was also scouting for Middlesbrough when Jack Charlton was the manager.'

It was 50 years ago that Ken played at Newcastle and things have changed a lot since his era. I asked him for his memories of St James' Park and the training regime.

Chapter I: KEN PRIOR

'The first thing that hit you in the stadium was the Popular Side. It seemed to gan back forever. It was just a sea of caps. Like I say, there were about 60,000 people in the ground when we played against Middlesbrough, but they were all standing and they were right on top of you. It's impossible to play well every game. If you weren't having a good game, or you were having a mediocre game, but you were trying, they knew and they used to cheer you on. It was really good. Then obviously on the other side there was the Paddock. It was 2/6d to get in there. The ground itself was just pretty basic. It was a run-of-the-mill First Division ground. I mean, there wasn't any one really better than the others – they were all like that. There were some slightly better than the others, but not a great deal. The pitch wasn't bad. I was talking to Ted Ditchburn, the Tottenham goalkeeper, in Portugal, and I says, "Ted, do you remember when we beat you 7–1 and you were in goal?" He says, "I know I was. The pitch was the fault there." I says, "Well, that's funny, cos Tottenham were playing on it an' all, like." He just started to laugh.

'I remember the bullring where we used to train through the week. We used to play on there and it was all little stones. We used to play five-a-side. That was part of the training, playing five-a-side on the bullring. But the training, we had to do laps round and round and we did a few sprints. It was not what it is nowadays. All the time that I was there – I was there nine seasons in two spells – the only time that I was injured, I did it myself. Nowadays I can't understand all these hamstring injuries that they get. I divvn't know what they do in training, I haven't a clue what they're doing. They're breaking down and I cannot understand it. I mean, there must be something going wrong somewhere. It's always the hamstring, you know. In my day they used to tackle you from behind, kick you up a height, and all sorts. I mean, I've had a few knocks and cuts. Those old leather balls, they couldn't kick one of them now.'

The build-up to a game at St James' Park has no doubt changed dramatically since Ken played for Newcastle United. He recalled what it was like in the Fifties.

'If we were at home, I used to have like a poached egg or something very light around about a quarter-past, half-past eleven. Then Jackie Milburn used to pick us up in his little Ford 'Ten' and away we used to gan. The best laugh I've ever had, we'd been playing at home against West Bromwich and we're coming out of the Haymarket. They had the tramlines in those days and this tram passed us. Jackie was driving and this fella jumped off the tram in front of us and Jackie hit him. We were coming up the hill out of the Haymarket, the hill's still there. Well, this polis came flying across and he opened the car door. He gans, "Oh, hello Jack, did you see that idiot jump off the tram?" Jack says, "Aye, what a stupid thing to do." Well, I was ill. I was sitting there thinking that we were going to get clattered. It was funny. We had some laughs.

'Funnily enough, I was nervous in the dressing room. I'll tell you what, we got introduced to the Australian cricket team one day. I thought that we were shaking hands with the elite. But as soon as we went out of the tunnel I was okay. I mean, to me it was just another game of football. It was quicker. At that particular time I was only training twice a week. It was a lot quicker. You had to like really suck your breath. But once you got into the game and used with the pace, then it was alright. I had a lot of help off Charlie Crowe and Jimmy Scoular. I used to bunk with Jimmy on the away games. He was like the elder statesman and I was the young 'un. He used to sort of look after you. It did you good.

'On match days we used to go to the County Hotel, straight opposite the railway station. We used to have a room there and everybody had like a sherry and egg and a bit of a chat about the game. It wasn't a tactical chat because there wasn't a coach as such. Norman Smith, a grand old fella, loved Norman, he just used to come in and say, "Watch this player, watch that player". He didn't involve me because he was mostly talking to the defence. He said that my job was getting down the line and getting the ball over. He used to say, "Let Robledo and Milburn do the rest. If you do that, get the ball across, then your job's done. Let them make the mistakes." I says, "Fair enough, that's an easy enough job." So that's what we did. Then we had a slow walk up to the ground, not in a group like, but in ones and twos. We'd gan out and have a look at the pitch to see what length of studs you had to knock on or take off, because they were the old-fashioned leather studs.

'We would gradually get ready and just wait 'til the referee says, "Right lads, out you go". That was it. There were no team talks or owt like that. I can't remember any anyway. In fact, there was nobody there to give a team talk. Stan Seymour used to come in if we were getting beat at half-time. He used to play war with us, one thing and another, and tell us what we were doing wrong. It's funny, everybody can tell you what you're doing wrong, but can't tell you how to put it right. You know what I mean? There were some funny people who were there at the time, but I liked Stan Seymour. He had me one night when he says, "Come here". I went across and he gave us a corner flag stick. He says, "Stick that on the penalty spot. Right, now I want you to take a corner kick and hit that stick. Then come into the dressing room when you've finished." I bet I took 50 of 'em before I went into the dressing room. He says, "How many times have you hit it?" I says, "Once". He says, "Yes, I know you have because I've been watching you, but you were getting closer all the time. On a Saturday, that's all I want you to do, drop the ball on the penalty spot. It's too far for the goalkeeper to come out. It's a very difficult ball to cover." So there weren't any hard and fast rules at training.

'We had a practice match once a week. We used to mix up all the players and after that it was just a bath and home. Then you used to gan in on a Friday morning and collect your money. That was your £18 and £4 for a win and £2 for a draw. Then George Eastham came and that was the beginning of the big money. My brother-in-law, Bobby Cowell, and me reckoned up once, he'd got three FA Cup final medals, he had 13 seasons there. They had a benefit match for him and he got £4,000, which was a mockery for the number of people that were there. Peter Beardsley made more in one week than Bob made in 13 seasons. It was hard to believe.'

Ken, like a lot of former Newcastle United players, used to go to St James' Park to watch home games, with provision being made for ex-employees. Even the former players of the club were destined to be affected by the changing nature of football and the big business that it had become.

'I've only ever seen one game in the new stadium. We used to have like a pass, well not a pass as such. There were 26 seats in the old Milburn Stand and we used to phone up on a Saturday. In fact, Bob used to get mine. I'd get my ticket but we still had to pay for it. The old players used to sit there, Frank; Charlie, a few more, Ronnie sometimes. When Fletcher came I got a letter saying that it had all been stopped. 26 out of 52,000 and they weren't even full every week. Some players were ill or couldn't get there, this, that and the other. I mean, I only used to gan about six or eight times a season. I picked my games to gan to. Then they stopped it. I said, "Right, that's me finished". And I've only been once and it was against Manchester City last season. I was speaking to John Hall the other night. I was very friendly with John. He was a centre-half as a junior, a good player. I think that he played for West Sleekburn Juniors. He had once told my sister that they were stopping the tickets. I mean, there was Joe Harvey, his wife, my sister, Bob and me, and Joe Harvey was once manager of the club.'

Most of Ken's goals for Newcastle United came when he was playing in the reserve team, but he did score three senior goals.

'I scored against West Brom at home. I scored at Derby and Liverpool. That was some game that one. We got beat 5–3. Stan Seymour came in before the game and he says to Ronnie Simpson,

Chapter I: KEN PRIOR

"Ronnie, the Scottish selectors are watching you today." That was the worst thing that he could ever tell him. Billy Liddle, the outside-left for Liverpool, went right down the by-line and hit the ball across, chest high. Ronnie caught it and walked back into the goal. You should've heard Joe Harvey. I'm nearly sure that we were the only team that season that scored three goals at Liverpool and got nothing. We didn't even get a point. I scored a few goals in the reserves and I scored a lot of goals when I was at Millwall.'

The 1950s will always be remembered for Newcastle United's three great FA Cup victories. Ken came agonisingly close to sharing in the glory of winning an FA Cup final medal.

'It was the 1952 FA Cup final against Arsenal and I was told at the beginning of the week that I was playing. Before the final, Newcastle had played Arsenal away and I played in that game. Jackie Milburn says, "Look, give yourself plenty of room, touch the ball past Wally Barnes and gan, because he'll never catch you." So this is what I did and I had a canny match. Everyone was patting us on the back. Jackie says, "You'll probably be in the final". I thought it was champion that I was going to get a Cup final medal. Anyway, to cut a long story short, I didn't play. Bobby Mitchell played and he was strapped up from his ankle to his thigh. He sold a dummy to Wally Barnes who did his knee with his studs. Wembley was terrible at one time for it and Wally did his knee, otherwise Mitchell would never have finished the game. Aye, I was told I was playing and then I think it was on the Friday before the game that I was told I wasn't playing. I got 10 quid. They reckon that was the value of the medal that they got at that particular time, £10. But that was as close as I ever came to playing in the FA Cup final.'

Ken played against some tough opponents and some were certainly larger than life.

'One of the hardest players that I played against was Foulkes of Manchester United. He was about six foot four, a massive lad. It was the Busby Babes team when they played up at Newcastle. It was Gordon Hughes' first game. But this Foulkes took some getting by. I remember Charlie Crowe saying, "Ken, I'll tell you what, when I get the ball, you go and I'll chip it over his head." This was at half-time. I says, "Charlie, he's six foot four. He's as quick as what I am. You're chipping it over his head and he's got five to 10 yards start on me. How far is the ball going to gan up in the air before it'll come down for me?" He was laughing. He says, "I see what you mean. Just give us the ball and I'll give you it back. We'll play the one-two." So Milburn scored that day and I think that we drew 1–1. That season, they were all killed in the Munich Air Disaster apart from Bobby Charlton and one or two others. I was very friendly with Duncan Edwards, he played right-half. I played against him in the reserves. We got to know each other through various games. He was killed. He was a good player.

'But the hardest player that I've ever played against was a full-back, Ron Flowers of Bolton Wanderers. He was a good player, a very hard player, but he was fair. When he tackled you, you knew that you'd been tackled. He was a smashing bloke. I think he was an international; he played along with Billy Wright. I played against some excellent players who at that time were quite famous.'

Looking back over his career, Ken found that it was not always necessarily the best thing to play for your local club.

'It was enjoyable; I really enjoyed it. I had 10 years full-time, something like that, then back onto part-time. Funnily enough, I was making more money playing part-time and working than I was playing full-time football. I went back to the pit. I was an electrician down the pit and I was playing for North Shields. I mean, money came into it, but you were only glad to be on the team sheet. I cannot understand these players who don't like playing in this or that position. I played in goal one day for Millwall against Watford. The goalkeeper was injured. The manager says, "You're in goal". When we were having a bit kick-in at training, I used to gan in goal and I enjoyed it.

'Looking back at the time I was at Newcastle and the time I was at Millwall, of the two I was probably happier at Millwall. If you were a local lad at Newcastle, they didn't seem to bother about you much. You see, when they brought George Eastham, he was well looked after because he was from Ireland, you see. When I finished training, I used to put my clothes on and gan home, along with a lad from Amble, and that was it. You used to look on the Thursday night to see if you were playing and where you were playing. You used to make your own way on a Saturday. You see, at Millwall I had digs that were very good and they seemed as if they were more interested in you. They were obliged to look after the digs lads, you see.

'Would I like to be playing today? If I had my time again, without a doubt. If I could start again and have the same time that I had, that would do me fine. Some of them today, when you see some of the things that they do, you wonder what they're thinking. They go down the line, the forwards rush in, and then they stop and come inside. As soon as they stop, if the defences are any good, they just step out and the forwards are left stranded. They are offside when the ball is crossed. Why don't they go at the full-back? They should try to beat them. If they cannot beat them, fair enough, but they should try to beat them. But they have their way of playing and I've got mine.'

During his time at St James' Park, Ken played in some tough games and against some equally tough opponents, but there was always time for some lighter moments.

'We were at the Station Hotel in Birmingham and Middlesbrough were staying in the same hotel. We were at the top end of the dining room and Middlesbrough were at the bottom end. They had a goalkeeper called Rolando Ugolini who was a known practical joker. He came up to our table and he puts his arms around Frank Brennan. He says, "Keep your eyes on Delapenha". Lindy Delapenha was the first Jamaican to play in the old English

First Division. So Ugolini went away into the foyer. It was a right posh place, the head waiter came in and he announces, "Mr Delapenha, you are required on the telephone in the foyer, telephone number two". So we all watched. He gets up and Ugolini had tied his shoelaces round the table leg. Down came the table and Ugolini's in the foyer hanging onto the door of the phone box. Delapenha's jumping mad. He couldn't get his shoes off the leg of the table. Why, we were ill, literally ill with laughter.

'Another time when we were in Blackpool, I remember Frank Brennan hated Gorgonzola cheese. We all came down and we were having breakfast, and there was no Brennan. I cannot be perfectly sure, but I think it was Tommy Casey who did it. Tommy came in last, you see. He sat down and he says, "Where's big Frank?" I says, "I don't know, I haven't seen him." Then the door's opened and in walks Brennan. Why, he was a mountain of a man. He's looking round and he says, "Who's done it?" Everybody's going "Done what?" In those days you used to put your shoes outside your room and they used to come and polish them. Somebody had stuffed Brennan's shoes with Gorgonzola cheese. Well, I was killing myself laughing. I'm sure that it was Casey who did it. He was a smashing lad.'

Ken's career at Newcastle United was no doubt stifled by the presence of Bobby Mitchell, who was selected ahead of him for first-team duty. However, Ken was still a talented player who went on to serve the North East well both as a player and as a manager. During his playing days Ken came up against some big lads but he held his own on the pitch. Mind you, I would imagine that during team photos he avoided standing next to Frank Brennan when the photographer announced, "Say cheese".

DAVE HOLLINS
(1961–67)

DAVID MICHAEL HOLLINS was born on 4 February 1938 in Bangor, North Wales. Signed from Brighton and Hove Albion in March 1961 for £11,000, Dave was a goalkeeper for Newcastle United, making 121 senior starts. Dave played for his country and gained 11 full caps as well as two Under-23 caps. His brother John played for Chelsea and another brother, Roy, played for Brighton.

Dave's football career started very much in a 'like father like son' way.

'Well, my father Bill was a professional footballer. He played for Wolves and Stoke City and of course he was a goalkeeper. So, I obviously just followed in his footsteps really. He was my guide and my mentor. It all started from there and at the age of 15 I found that I was playing in a men's league, albeit as a very slender lad. It was a really good apprenticeship because in those days it was highly physical. Goalkeepers were quite vulnerable physically, but I came through and at the age of 18, I went for a trial at Brighton. They accepted me and I was an apprentice. It probably took me three or four years to make my full debut. I was at Brighton for about six and a half years and then in 1961, I was transferred to Newcastle.'

The world of football has changed much since Dave was a young lad and the players are much more in the spotlight nowadays.

'There weren't many heroes really because football in those days wasn't projected as much as it is now. You never had *Match of the Day* or anything like that. There wasn't a great deal other than when you would read things in the newspapers. So, they were pretty ancient days. There were no great heroes, but there were some great footballers around at the time.'

Dave spent several years playing at Brighton before his dramatic move north to St James' Park. His debut for Newcastle United was in a somewhat surprising away victory at White Hart Lane against Tottenham Hotspur, during which he dramatically saved a penalty. His home debut was to prove equally as dramatic, with him letting in six goals in front of an expectant Toon Army.

'Well, according to the manager of Brighton and Hove Albion, 15 to 20 years later, he had a choice. In those days you never had a choice as a player, you either went or you didn't go to certain clubs. So, there were two clubs in the market, one was Everton and the other one was Newcastle. He chose Newcastle for me. I actually signed in a hotel at Kings Cross, that was where I signed. Then I stayed in a hotel near the station in Newcastle, an old hotel. After that I was in digs. My wife was expecting a baby. Bob Stokoe had just been transferred, he had just gone, and I was able to take over his club house. So I moved into his club house and I had Len White living just round the corner in Fenham. So I didn't have to stay in digs for very long.

'I remember Bobby Moncur being there in the same digs. Bobby Moncur was a player who I admired very much because he reminded me a lot of my younger brother at the age of 15 and 16. His dedication and his willpower to do well, they were very similar, and they both succeeded in playing at the top level, not only for their clubs but also for their country.

'My debut was in 1961 at Tottenham. It is one of my greatest memories really because I felt as though I was walking on water. Everything that I did came off. I really enjoyed it. That was the year that Tottenham won the double and I don't think they'd lost a game in two years at White Hart Lane. Danny Blanchflower took the penalty, so that was special. My home debut against Chelsea was unbelievable for very different reasons. Jimmy Greaves literally ripped us apart on his own. He scored four goals. He was a great player, a wonderful player. I think that there were 30,000 people there. We were never in it. They basically played the game in our 18-yard box.'

Not long after Dave had joined Newcastle United, the club was relegated to the old Second Division, but the writing was very much on the wall by the time he arrived at St James' Park. However, he had great memories of the club and the supporters.

'I think that there were probably about 10 games to go, or maybe less than that when I arrived, so they were already doomed. It was a wonderful stadium and the atmosphere…I mean, I played at Liverpool and I even played in the Maracana Stadium in Brazil,

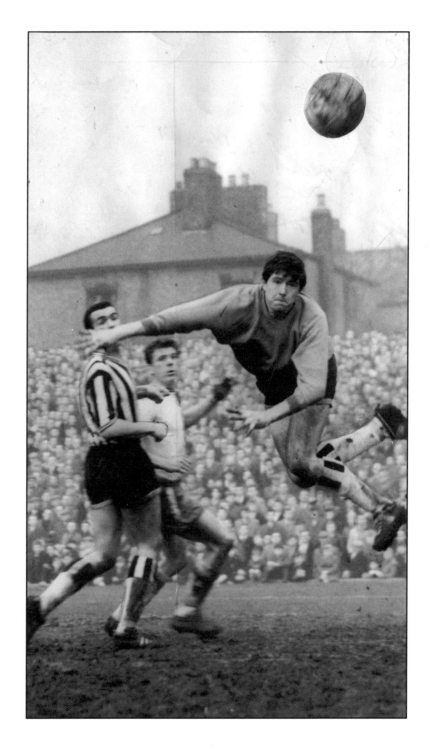

where there were 222,000, but there was no atmosphere like the Gallowgate. The crowd was fantastic, they were magical. I don't think I have ever come across other supporters that could create that atmosphere, including Liverpool.'

Being a goalkeeper, I asked Dave about his recollections of training and matchday preparations.

'Training was very minimal. Basically the goalkeeper always trained with the outfield players. There was no specialised goalkeeping training or coaching. But, what I used to do, I used to stay behind half an hour after the regular training had finished. There was a young lad, a young apprentice called Pop Robson, who used to stay back with me. I think that was probably how he became such a good predator, a good striker. He went on and had a very good career.

'On matchdays, on arrival, probably an hour or an hour and a half before the match, there were thousands of people there. To park the car then go through the crowds was terrific. Everybody was asking for autographs. You would arrive and say hello to different people. If you wanted a bit of a massage, which was pretty rare, you would go to your place and go through your normal routine. I think that I used to get a bit of a hiccup, which was a bit of a nervous thing that used to happen. The dressing rooms were quite big and very well organised. There was always a great deal of banter, a great deal of joke telling. There was a player there, Bill McKinney, who was a full-back, a local lad, who always used to be the life and soul of the party. I used to get fairly nervous, but it was nothing really. Having a father who was an ex-professional, he learned me all the do's and don'ts. Everybody reacts in a different way, nervously. A few of the lads used to like a drop of brandy before going out, they used to knock some of that down. Everyone had a different approach.'

When I asked Dave to recall some of his more memorable games playing for Newcastle United, it was perhaps inevitable that he would start with his debut in the away game against Tottenham.

'I think that was probably the best one, my debut. I was in awe of so many of my team colleagues. I was in awe of Ivor Allchurch and Len White and a few others, Alf McMichael, Dick Keith. There were some wonderful internationals, some great players. I think that would be the greatest memory. Also, there were the derby matches with Sunderland. We always seemed to draw 1–1. The results were nearly always 1–1.

'My brother John and I played against one another in the old First Division. One game was Newcastle at Stamford Bridge, Chelsea. It was on 25 September 1965 and the score was 1–1. John was desperate to score. We were both captains for the day. I was actually taken off with concussion following a collision with George Graham, who was the centre-forward. But we managed to get through with a 1–1 draw. So that was a great family event.'

As well as some great memories, Dave also recalled another one from his career that he would rather have forgotten.

'Yes, I do. It might have been in the FA Cup or in the League; it was at Blackpool. I had to come into the side because every goalkeeper was injured. I'd had the flu and, well, I had to play really. I was the only one who was still standing on two feet. So, we went down to Blackpool and we got beat 6–0, and that was truly horrendous. That was not a good game at all. Maybe I shouldn't have played but I was the only one left. Everyone else was injured.

'I did have the pleasure of playing against Stanley Matthews. I can remember making a couple of saves from shots by Stanley Matthews when he was playing at Stoke City. I can also remember Jackie Milburn, he was writing for the *News of the World* at the time, he used to come onto the pitch. It would be just after a practice match and of course he would love getting the ball at his feet, and this wasn't even in a match. Jackie hit one on the volley from 25 or maybe 30 yards and I went up and pushed it over the bar. That was fantastic. To save one from Jackie Milburn was quite memorable because he really could hit the ball, even when he had his shoes on. So, that was one for the book. It's very difficult to memorise all these games, there were so many.'

Dave's affection for the Newcastle United supporters remains just as strong as when he was at St James' Park.

'They haven't changed, nowadays when you see them on the television, they haven't changed at all. They are just fanatical. I've been on holiday, I was in Bali on holiday, and this chap came up to me out of nowhere and how on earth he recognised me I don't know, but he knew me. He came from Bedlington, Bill Thompson's area, and I spent nearly all the holiday talking to him about past games. He recognised me and I was miles and miles away from anywhere. That is what Newcastle United supporters are like, they never forget. I see them down here even when I'm playing bowls and they know me. I am waiting to go to Cyprus where there are a lot of ex-pats and a lot of Newcastle United supporters. I am going to meet some of them through a friend of mine. They keep saying, "You've got to come over".'

Dave played for Wales and gained 11 full caps. Playing for his country was a proud achievement that he still cherishes.

'My father was gradually finishing his career playing for Bangor City in North Wales and that's where I was born. So it was a birthright. While I was playing for Brighton, I managed to play for the Welsh Under-23s and progressed on to full internationals. Fortunately I played with Ivor Allchurch, Ken Leek, Ollie Burton, Wyn Davies, all the good old Newcastle players. I never played against my brother John at international level. It would have been a tremendous story if we had. It's a very rare thing really to have two brothers play for different countries.

'It was a great experience, especially with Ivor Allchurch being at the club. To go away with him was special and I really had some wonderful trips. But I think that my greatest memory, I've already mentioned it, was playing at the Maracana Stadium in Brazil. I think that Ken Leek was also playing, he was a centre-forward for Newcastle United. I was on the bench, substitute goalkeeper, but the 'keeper was badly injured so I came on and that was the start of my international career. That was also the start of Pele's career. He was 17 years old. He scored two goals and one of them was a header. He outjumped John Charles who was six foot four or five and everybody thought who the hell is this? He became a world legend.'

The conversation inevitably turned to the subject of formidable opponents at this time and Dave recalled quite a few. He also revealed that he always did his homework before meeting them on the pitch.

'Jimmy Greaves, Denis Law, George Best, Bobby Charlton, now he was something special, especially if he had a chance of scoring; he was pretty lethal. But there were so many others. What I used to do was, whatever division I was playing in, I always had a little book that I used to keep a check on players. I would keep a note of the penalty takers, people who would be physical, right foot, left foot. It was a thing that my father taught me to do. You couldn't always rely on your memory. Len White was a very powerful kicker of the ball, a very strong player. I was very disappointed that they didn't call him up for England. He was also a very nice chap. But there you are. That was how things were. He certainly would have been called up if he was playing nowadays.'

Dave played under three different managers during his time at St James' Park and was clearly saddened when things started to go wrong for him.

'So, who did we have? We had Charlie Mitten, we had Norman Smith, so there was probably a two-year period before Joe Harvey came along. All managers will clear players out and bring in their own players. When Joe bought Gordon Marshall, who was over six foot tall, it certainly created some competition for the jersey. But it's a normal thing to do. I was disappointed to leave because I really loved playing up there. I was still there for a long time.'

Chapter 2: DAVE HOLLINS

It was clear that Dave really enjoyed his playing days with Newcastle United and he recalled some fond memories. He also remembered that being in the Newcastle squad could be an interesting and entertaining adventure.

'Well, I think what was an eye-opener for me was when I had made my debut and we had beaten Tottenham at White Hart Lane 2–1. We went to Kings Cross station to catch the sleeper to go back to Newcastle and I was sitting in one of the carriages with some of the lads. All of a sudden these crates of beer started to appear and I remember saying "Who are these for?" "Oh, they're for us" came the reply from somebody. They were full of bottles of Newcastle Brown Ale. I couldn't believe it, but it was all part and parcel of an away match. By the time we got to Darlington a few of the lads were a bit under the weather. But that all comes under the heading of team spirit. It was brilliant.

'There were a lot of characters. Barrie Thomas, a prolific goalscorer, if you put him in front of goal, with an open goal, he would miss. He could put them in from any angle, a bit like Kerry Dixon of Chelsea, he would score from anywhere. As a goalkeeper you would think, well he's not going to shoot from there. But he does and of course you're not ready for it. Your angles are not right and it goes in. So that was Barrie.'

I asked Dave if he had his time all over again whether or not he would have liked to be playing nowadays.

'I would love to do that. I have got great admiration for the goalkeeper who is playing at Newcastle now, Shay Given. I mean, he is small compared to many others but he reads the game so well. His positional play is excellent. For me, I would say that he is the best goalkeeper in the Premier League. We have got lots of good goalkeepers, English goalkeepers who play in the lower divisions, but they are just not recognised. The only one who impresses me today, as I said, is the Newcastle lad, and I do know that he is Irish. He is so dependable.

'I remember that we always went to a men's tailors and bought these string gloves. They were aerated, they had holes in them so that the warmth of your hands dried them out. I found them to be quite efficient. These modern day gloves are huge. As a goalkeeper you have got eight yards to cover. It is such a specialised position that you have got to know every angle. So the penalty spot and the near post are always your guide. In that respect, nothing has changed. As a goalkeeper, you still have to get it all right.'

Dave was transferred to Mansfield Town in February 1967 for £11,000, being disappointed to leave St James' Park after six memorable years. Dave's career with Newcastle United started with a famous penalty save that made him an instant hit with the supporters. He was then hit for six by Chelsea. Fortunately for Dave, John was not yet playing for them. If he had been, I wonder who would have said 'Oh brother!'

Chapter 3

KEITH KETTLEBOROUGH
(1966)

KEITH FRANK KETTLEBOROUGH was born on 29 June 1935 in Rotherham, Yorkshire. Keith was a shrewd short-term purchase from Sheffield United in January 1966, costing Newcastle United £22,500. He was a midfield player who only stayed for one year, but made a vital contribution that should never be underestimated.

Although Keith was successful at football, it was not his first love when he was a child.

'When I was a kid growing up, the game that I actually loved was cricket. In fact, at the age of 14, I used to catch the old tram out of All Saints Square in Rotherham and travel up to Sheffield. I used to walk up to Bramall Lane in Sheffield and watch Yorkshire and whoever they were playing against. There were people like Len Hutton, Maurice Leyland and people like that. So cricket was actually my first love.

'At 14 years of age I played with Yorkshire Schoolboys, who in those days only had one Under-15 team. Now I believe that Yorkshire Schoolboys have several teams – Under-13, 14, 15 and so on. I played for two years and in the next year I played for the North of England against the South. There were people like Ken Taylor who, incidentally, I played against at football when he was at Huddersfield. So it was cricket really. Everyone thought that I was going to play cricket. But I was a little on the small side and I went for trials for Rotherham schoolboys at football. I got changed and went down to where they were holding the trials. The master in charge took one look at me and he said, "Oh, you can go, you're too small." So I didn't bother a lot with football at that time. I played with the school team and that kind of thing. Then I played for the local YMCA team, Rotherham YMCA, in the local leagues.

'Then I did my National Service and it was just as I was getting demobbed, out at a place called Mantby near Louth in Lincolnshire, that a Grimsby Town scout had been watching me play with the camp side on occasions. So he invited me to Grimsby for trials. I had a fortnight there. I thought that I'd done alright and my wife also thought that I'd done alright. But they wanted me to stay for another fortnight. They had given me £3 spending money and paid for my digs for the fortnight. I mean, that might sound a bit ludicrous, but I suppose a pint of beer was only about five pence at that time. I had no job to come back to. I decided that where I was working before I went into the RAF, there wasn't enough money in it and I decided that I was going to have a change. So I said, "No, I'm not prepared to stop on, I'm off back home."

'So I came back home to Rotherham and, of course, you know how news travels in football, I started playing with the YMCA team again. Then a fella called Portman, who was scouting for Rotherham United, came to see me and invited me down to Millmoor to Rotherham for a trial. I played three 18-team matches and the manager, Andy Smailes, signed me full-time. That was in December 1955. I played in one reserve match and then he pushed me straight into a cup-tie against Scunthorpe United. So within six weeks of playing on Ainthorpe playing fields, local playing fields, playing with the Rotherham YMCA team, I was playing in a third round cup-tie. Actually, I was a bit out of my depth for a start. I had a good time with Rotherham reserves for a season and a half before I established myself as a player.

'I was at Rotherham until 1960 and then John Harris, the manager of Sheffield United, came along. At that time, there was a Sheffield and District team that played against the Football Federation in Scotland, a Glasgow side. The Sheffield side had players picked from Sheffield United, Sheffield Wednesday, Barnsley, Doncaster and Rotherham. I played in one of those matches in Glasgow where John Harris was the team manager. He took me to one side and asked if I was interested in going to Bramall Lane to play for Sheffield United. So they talk nowadays about tapping players up, but it's been going on for years and years. Anyway, I said that I was interested and about three or four weeks later he came along with his chairman and I signed for Sheffield United. I had six good years there. I enjoyed playing there. We got promotion at the end of the first season that I was there and we were in what is now the Premiership, the old First Division. I really enjoyed it, playing against people like Bobby Moore and George Best.

'At that time, tactics were not exactly non-existent, but there were not a lot of managers who were using different tactics. We had not worked on anything. We were playing Manchester United at Old Trafford and John Harris came to me at a quarter to three and says, "I want you to pick up George Best". And my reaction was, what about Bobby Charlton, what about Paddy Crerand? George Best, I never got near to him. For what it's worth, in my opinion, I think that he was the best footballer that these four countries of ours have ever produced. I remember seeing people like Peter Docherty, Wilf Mannion, Stanley Matthews, you know, and then John Charles of course later on. But I thought that Bestie was a better player. He didn't ever fulfil his full potential in my opinion.'

Before transferring to Newcastle United, Keith was on the fringe of full international experience.

'I was in Alf Ramsey's shadow England squad in 1965 for the Austria match. Alf used to pick 22 players at that time. There were no substitutes at that time. I was in his shadow squad for the Austria match and I enjoyed that. That was a nice experience. It was the only time that I got to walk out onto the pitch at Wembley, and I took it. I was a bit disappointed with the dressing rooms and the seating accommodation. They were a little bit sparse for what had become the national stadium. Then I had a knee injury – I did my cartilage. I had to have a cartilage taken out and it was four months before I played again. I started training and the knee blew up. They did different things with it, but nothing seemed to work and I just had to play with a floating kneecap, so to speak. It still swells up now. I think of some people who have reached my age and I'm great really, you know. But that's the only problem that I've got, my knee.'

Keith signed for Newcastle United in January 1966 and at that time he was ready for a new challenge.

Chapter 3: KEITH KETTLEBOROUGH

'Well, John Harris just came to me and said, "Newcastle are interested in you. Are you interested in going?" Things weren't going very well for him at that time at Bramall Lane. After six years, as you know, people can get a bit…Well, I suppose complacency sets in and I thought I was ready for a change. So I said, "Yes, I'm interested in going." I talked to Joe Harvey and we agreed terms. I came up and I think the first match that I played in was against West Ham. I'll never forget it, I came up on the Friday and I stayed at the County Hotel. Anyway, I was right above the dance floor and they were doing the "March of the Mods" at bloody one o'clock in the morning. I went into the ground the next day and I had a walk out on the pitch. It was like a blooming hayfield. Do you remember they used to put straw down? It was just like a hayfield. They raked it all off before we played, but of course you don't get it all off. I thought, "oh my god". But I think that we beat West Ham that day. Did we beat them 2–1?

'But it opened my eyes coming to Newcastle. Having played in my local area, South Yorkshire, for Rotherham and Sheffield United, I have to say that the fans up there in Newcastle are so great. They are different to what they are in this area. I mean, footballers up there are treated like gods, aren't they? In this area you only have to have a bad game and if you go out for a drink, you can see people whispering in the pubs, that kind of thing. But up there the fans were marvellous. I have to say, I wasn't right impressed with the way the football club was run. In fact I didn't rate Joe Harvey as a good manager. Joe was a funny sort of character, but we got on alright. He treated everybody alright. There were no problems in that respect. As I say, tactically he was a bit unwise. In fact, the best manager I ever worked with, as far as football knowledge was concerned, was Jimmy McGuigan at Chesterfield.

'As for St James' Park, where you came out of the tunnel, the opposite side was all open. You could see a big Leech's sign in the distance, advertising Leech's buildings. I watched the programme on Bobby Robson on the telly recently and that stadium looks very impressive now, very impressive. I think that most football pitches are much improved nowadays, going by what you see on the telly. I mean, Old Trafford at times looks a blooming mess. But the rest of them, when you see them on the telly, they do seem to have improved a lot. The one at Rotherham, I remember playing in a cup-tie against Brighton and there was a stream across the bottom penalty area. It had a bit of a slope. I don't know if you've ever been to Millmoor, it was just a slight slope. It wasn't really noticeable from the terraces. When you were attacking that end, you got to the edge of the penalty area in the game and it just stopped. But they got rid of that and the pitch is in fair condition now. Sadly the actual ground is abysmal.'

When Keith arrived at St James' Park, Newcastle United were struggling to avoid getting sucked into a relegation battle in the old First Division. He was brought in to provide strength in midfield. I asked for his memories of the team at that time.

'Jimmy Greenhaugh was the trainer, coach, or whatever you want to call him. Jimmy was okay; he was quite good. I remember people like Alan Suddick, who had a tremendous amount of ability but he didn't always use it. In fact, I think the idea was he would only have the ball in their half of the field. In our half, if he got the ball, he was likely to lose it and get you in trouble. I remember Pop Robson was just coming through as a youngster as well. Really, on paper it wasn't a bad side, but we did struggle to stay in that First Division. There were people like Ron McGarry who were great to get on with, but they seemed to be a set of players who were very much individuals at that time.

'I don't know if I read it wrong, but the impression I got was that there was a lack of team cohesion. I suppose I had a fairly sheltered life football-wise with Rotherham and Sheffield United, where there were a lot of local lads in both sides. To my mind, at Rotherham and Sheffield we were more of a team than at

Newcastle. Whether I'd read it wrong, with only being there a short time, I don't know, but that was the impression that I left with. And that was a bad move that I made, leaving Newcastle United. I came back to Doncaster Rovers as player-manager and I think that it was after five months, they kicked me out of the front door. George Raynor, the little fella who took Sweden into the World Cup, well he had his hand on the back door, so to speak. They'd got him lined up before I went. But, to be fair, I made one or two mistakes there. We were in the old Third Division and they were in a bad way when I got there, and I accepted the fact that I was prepared to go down and start again. But the directors didn't see it like that and I made a mistake in telling them that we were going to go down. That was with about eight or nine matches to play. So my head was on the block and they chopped it off.

'But then I went to Chesterfield and I had a couple of very happy years there. I played in all four divisions, you know, before I finished with football. When I finished at Chesterfield, I went to Matlock in Derbyshire, who were then in what was the Northern Premier League. It became the Unibond and it's now all part of the pyramid. I had about 18 months there that I enjoyed. I went into business and I packed in playing football. I was about 39 at the time and that was that. I don't watch football now. I'd sooner play golf on a Saturday afternoon.'

Keith's contribution to the fight against relegation in the 1965–66 season was crucial in many ways and his midfield skills had a major impact on the fortunes of the club at the time. Keith seemed to be quite modest about his performances and acknowledged that he was distracted.

'I don't remember too many games, not really. I know that it was a battle. I think that we went to Tottenham and got a point, things like that. Nothing really sticks out. Oh, and then I had a great cricket season with Chester-le–Street in the Durham City League. It might sound crazy, but the cricket season was more enjoyable than the football. In fact, there they had a fella at the time called Russell Inglis and I think he was one of the best all-rounders that I've played league cricket with.'

Keith was only at St James' Park for a short time and he took a risk by moving on.

'When I came to Newcastle, I started off in the hotel and then I got a house behind the Lambton Worm pub in Chester-le-Street. It was all enjoyable and I wouldn't change anything really. I moved on because I got a little bit ambitious and this job came up. I could've either gone to Workington as player-manager or Doncaster Rovers. I mean, Workington was an out-of-the-way place, you know, and Doncaster, I was coming back into my own area, the area that I knew and the players who I knew. So I came back here to my own area and I fell between two stools with the board of directors. There was a bit of a power battle going on. From what I could gather, the chairman that brought me in wanted me and the fella that ousted him didn't want me. As I say, I fell between two stools.

'You get some good football matches up there at Newcastle, don't you? You've got to be content with being in the Premiership and doing reasonably well. There can only be four successful teams in that League; the four who get into the Champions League. Looking back, I enjoyed my football career, wherever I played.'

Keith Kettleborough still holds the record for being the player with the longest surname ever to play for Newcastle United. The cost of a replica shirt bearing his name nowadays would not come cheap. Keith still remembers the words of manager Joe Harvey when he signed for Newcastle United. He said, 'I'm going to sign a big name'.

Chapter 4

JIM SCOTT
(1967–70)

JAMES SCOTT was born in Falkirk, Scotland, on 21 August 1940. Playing in midfield or as an outside-right, Jim was transferred to Newcastle United from Hibernian in August 1967 for £35,000. He made 92 senior starts for the club and scored 12 goals. He also gained one full international cap. Jim was a prominent member of the Newcastle United squad that won the Inter Cities Fairs Cup in

1969. You could say that Jim's love of football was very much a family affair.

'Well, I think so. It was my father's doing. There were three of us, three brothers. My father played and all three of us followed in his footsteps. My football hero as a child was obviously Stanley Matthews. He was the main one who comes to mind, but there were a few others. I can go back to when I was at school and I could tell you players who played in every team in Scotland in the late 1940s and early 1950s. I couldn't tell you who played there last year. Every club at that particular time had five or six players who you could remember because they could really play. But I couldn't tell you who played for them last year.

'If you were good at football, you would hope to play for your school team in your last year at primary school. I played the last two years. Then I went to the secondary school. From there I played with Denny in what they used to call under-age juveniles. From there I went to Bo'ness and I was there for a season, although I had signed provisional with Hibernian. I went to Hibs and they tried me out against Hearts' reserves, with maybe about two months of the season to go, or maybe even less, six weeks. I'll always remember the left-back, Tom McKenzie, he was a stalwart with Hearts, and I really gave him a good chasing. And I never looked back. I played with the reserve team and all of a sudden I found myself in the first team. In fact I remember I played in a reserve-team game at Motherwell and the chairman of the club was Harry Swan at the time. I was only a lad, I think I was barely 18. I don't think I was 18, I think I was only 17. Anyway, Harry Swan came in after the game and he says to me, "Report to Easter Road on Saturday." I says, "Mr Swan, I cannot because I'm playing with Bo'ness." He says, "Don't worry about that, I'll sort that out." I was only a kid, you know. That was the start of me playing for Hibs.'

Jim transferred to Newcastle United in 1967 after several seasons with Hibernian. It was a move that he felt ready for.

'Well, actually I played in a charities game and it was a Hearts and Hibs Select team against Newcastle United. It must have been about 1958 and I remember that Joe Harvey played. I think that they had Ronnie Simpson in goal, Dick Keith was the right-back and Alf McMichael played at outside-right. And I think that we beat them 4–3. I scored a good goal. I think that was possibly always in their minds. As I said, Joe Harvey played that day and I think that the inside-forward was Len White. There were a few there who were well known. I think Jimmy Scoular played that day as well and the centre-half was Frank Brennan.

'I remember when Newcastle made the call. It was the pre-season, so I was training with Hibs. I got a phone call to say go down to Newcastle the next day. I'd wanted to leave Hibs earlier because I'd been there for nine years and I felt as though I was just built in with the bricks. For me, it was a chance to get away from there. I just went down and I was quite impressed with Newcastle. I liked Joe Harvey, I liked the man, so I was quite happy to move there. The wages were going up a bit, so I was very happy.'

The St James' Park that Jim moved to in 1967 was somewhat different to the one that stands proudly overlooking the city of Newcastle today.

'To be fair, going back, the old stadium was probably a better atmosphere. You would get 60,000 people in there and I think that it was a much better atmosphere. Of course, on the terraces there in those days you were standing up. It's certainly better going to a football match now than it was then.

'But you cannot stand now and I think a lot of the supporters miss that. I've been down there quite a few times to the new one and it's absolutely enormous. To think, you're saying to yourself, there are only 52,000 people in there, but you're forgetting that they are all seated. It's a terrific stadium, there's no question about that. It looks great. It's very impressive. It should be because of the supporters they've got. Newcastle should be winning things, you know. They should be up there winning things with the support that they've got.'

Having moved to the First Division in England, I asked Jim for his memories of training and match days with Newcastle United.

'We used to train at a stadium somewhere along the Scotswood Road and also up past the barracks at Hunters Moor. The training was okay. You trained hard, but you didn't get a lot of the ball. Nowadays it is probably very different. It was enjoyable but you didn't get a lot of ball work. On match days, the thing is, when you played away you were there on the bus or the train. You were staying in a hotel. I used to room with Jackie Sinclair. He used to get up early in the morning and go for a walk. I stayed in my bed a lot longer, but everybody's different. Match days at home, you didn't get together in those days; you just had to report at the ground at two o'clock, that sort of thing. Nowadays they will go for a meal. The only time that we went for a meal, well I say the only time, it was every second week because you were away from home. But for home games, you just reported at two o'clock. There was nothing special for me, not really, no superstitions. I never thought about it, I just thought about the game.'

Jim made his debut for Newcastle United on 19 August 1967 playing against Southampton at St James' Park. It was the first game of the new season with Newcastle winning 3–0.

'I can remember my debut very well because we played against Southampton and it was 0–0 at half-time. Pop Robson was our substitute that day. I had a bit of a weight problem when I went down to Newcastle because I was on tour in America and I was about a stone and three pounds overweight. I took it off and I didn't think that I was going to make the start of the season. But I did make the start and I had got the excess weight off. I remember looking at the touchline and seeing Pop Robson getting warmed up and I wasn't having such a good debut. And I thought to myself, there is only one person coming off here and that was me. But I managed to rattle in the first goal and after that I sort of played a bit better. That first goal certainly helped. I had thought that there was only one person coming off. I can remember it as though it was yesterday.'

The goal scored by Jim against Southampton helped Newcastle United to victory at the start of the 1967–68 season and it also salvaged his debut performance. Jim developed a habit of scoring crucial goals for the club and it was he who scored Newcastle's first ever goal in a European competition at the start of the successful Inter Cities Fairs Cup campaign in 1968, netting against Feyenoord in the first round, first leg at St James' Park.

'I remember that one as well. Geoff Allen, he had a super game that night, he sent the ball across and I scored the first goal. Actually, I think if you look back, I was the first substitute to come on for Newcastle and score. I think that was at Coventry, if you look that one up. I think we beat Coventry 4–1 and I scored the first goal that day. I came on for Albert Bennett. Albert had done his cartilage. I think if you check that, you might find that I'm right that I was the first substitute to score for Newcastle.

'I can remember that we played Real Zaragoza away on New Year's Day. That would have been 1969. That was the away leg and we had to play on New Year's Day. I remember that we got beat 3–2 that day. Of course, 3–2 was quite a good score away from home, you know. I think we beat them 2–1 at home and went through on the away goals rule.

I can remember the Zaragoza games. Actually I can remember them all, all the games in the Fairs Cup. Playing against Rangers, that was a good one for me and for Jackie Sinclair because we scored the goals and, coming from Scotland, it was a bit of a bonus. It was a hard game up until we scored. I don't think I'd ever scored a better goal. Tommy Gibb shoved the ball inside of the full-back and I just hit it. It just slammed into the back of the net. Jackie got the second one. It was quite a good feeling that we beat them because when I played for Hibs up in Scotland, we hardly ever beat Rangers.'

Football has changed a lot since Jim's playing days and he reflected upon his era compared to modern times.

'When I played football I never had a bad game, I've just got a bad memory. I mean, you would never get a player who could go through the whole season without having a bad spell. There would be times on the park when you couldn't kick a ball. There would be other times when you couldn't do anything wrong. That's the way it was. I think there's certainly been an improvement in the game and with the ball as well. It seems easier to get the ball nowadays. Football today, I was talking to the lads in the pub about it the other day. There was a programme on the telly about the Fairs Cup Final against Ujpesti Dozsa and Bob Moncur was on it. The programme showed you about 20 minutes of the first game and 20 minutes of the second one. You know, there were fouls going in all over the place, but there was nobody trying to get anybody sent off. There was not one person who argued with the referee. Obviously, the referee was a referee and he gave some bad decisions then, just as they do now, but nobody argued with him. They just got on with the game.

'Nowadays they are diving about all over the place and they are trying to get people sent off. Honestly, I hate to say this but football used to be an exciting game. To me, all the excitement in a football match should be in the penalty box. The only time you see players in the penalty box now is for a free-kick or a corner-kick. To me that's where all the action should be. I'm not saying that every game is like that. I think you are swamped with television as well today. It's not good enough; the games are not good enough. Sometimes you watch a game for five minutes and you think to yourself, this is not going to get any better. And you keep watching it and it doesn't get any better.

'Certainly the game down in England is much harder than it is up in Scotland. They get a hard game in the Premier League every week whether they are bottom of the League or top of the League. I'm not saying it's not exciting, but a lot of the games just aren't as exciting as they used to be. As I say, you didn't see people trying to get others sent off or going to the referee saying that someone should get a yellow card. I mean, in our day as well, when somebody got sent off, it was headlines in the newspaper. Nowadays, if they finish a game with 11 men on the pitch they've done well. I can certainly remember seeing the headlines in the papers in Scotland when somebody got sent off, but it was very unusual.'

As he recalled the nature of the game in his era, Jim highlighted the physical side of it. I asked him if he had any particular opponents who he found difficult. He gave a special mention to a player who was very close to home.

'To be honest, I didn't really bother myself worrying about defenders. But I played against the best, such as Cooper and McNab, and I loved playing against them. You know, the boy I could never play against was Ron Guthrie. Ron couldn't get a game at Newcastle because he couldn't get chosen ahead of Frank Clark. If ever we had a practice game, Joe Harvey would come and say, "Right, the first-team forwards will play against the reserve-team defence." The lad, Ron, always used to know where I was because he just knew everything about me. I just couldn't play against him. And yet, when he did get in the first team, he just couldn't do it. He went on to Sunderland and he won an FA Cup medal.'

The wages paid out to the modern-day players are so far removed from the days when Jim was at St James' Park and this has inevitably affected the lifestyles of the current crop. Jim reflected on these changes.

'Well, I think it's the wages that have changed everything. Don't get me wrong, if that is what they are getting, £15–20,000 a week, if I was a top-class player, that is what I'd be wanting. But I think now, they've jumped into the superstar bracket and they are like actors and film stars. But I think that their social lives suffer because they cannot do anything. If they go into the back of a nightclub and pee in the toilet, somebody's likely there to take their photograph. It is like living in a goldfish bowl. I think it is how the fans see them. The last time I was down, when Bob Moncur had invited me down to the hospitality table for ex-players, another thing that I noticed when we were coming out was that the players now come out from under the stand in their cars. People are waiting to see them and they just wave. It is so impersonal. When we came out of the old stadium, my wife would be sitting in the car waiting for me. It would probably take me 20 minutes or more to get to the car, signing autographs, you know. Nowadays the fans don't get that opportunity. I don't know if it's wrong but that's just the way it is.'

When Jim was playing for Newcastle United, the manager throughout his stay was Joe Harvey. Jim had a lot of respect for the man.

'Joe, I got on well with him. He was a man's man and you could always speak to him. I remember when he dropped me and he brought in Jackie Sinclair. Jackie came as an outside-right and he put him in the side at the start of the season. I remember John McNamee had done my ankle in pre-season training, so I wasn't playing, I was just watching. And I came back and I played a couple of games for the reserve team. Jackie was playing absolutely terrible, so I went in to see Joe. I says, "Joe, Jackie is my best mate, but he is bloody terrible. As far as I'm concerned, I'm just about finished at the club." I just walked out, I went up the road, and I says to my wife, "Well, that's us finished. We'll be on that road now."

'That was on the Thursday, I think. I went down for the training on the Friday morning and did the training. I looked down at the reserves teamsheet and I thought, "Jesus Christ, I'm not even playing in the reserves." We were playing against Sunderland the next day at Roker Park. I was just going to walk away when I looked at the first-team list and I saw that I was playing. But actually, it was one of the best games that I ever played in for Newcastle. We drew 1–1 and there was a wee referee, Kevin, who came from Doncaster. It was Colin Todd who was right-back and he shoved the ball back to Montgomery. I nipped in and scored and the referee disallowed it. It was all over the Sunday papers. They kept showing it and showing it and the referee was wrong.

'Funnily enough, when I played with Crystal Palace, I trained with them in the February and I travelled there on the train on the Tuesday and I travelled back up on the Saturday to Newcastle until the end of the season. Who did I get coming back on the train? It was Kevin the referee. We used to have a bottle of beer and he would say, "I'm sorry. I was wrong." I just used to say, "Well, everybody does that sometime, Kevin." He was actually a smashing lad and I got on really well with him. He got off the train at Doncaster and I stayed on until Newcastle.'

Jim left Newcastle United in February 1970, when he was transferred to Crystal Palace, and he knew that his time had come to move on.

'I loved it down there, I really did. I didn't really want to go, but I think when the club no longer wants you, then that is it. Unfortunately, you cannot be there forever, it was just time for me to go. What convinced me was when we played against South-ampton in the Fairs Cup, down at Southampton. There was a squad of about 17 or 18, something like that anyway. We were training and that, and when they announced the team, there was me and Benny Arentoft, who had played in the final, who weren't even on the subs bench. I kind of thought that it was time to go.'

Jim retired from playing professional football after returning to Scotland and he has been running a pub in Falkirk. At the time of our conversation, Jim was contemplating his next retirement.

'I've got Aitkens Bar in Falkirk but I'm just about retired. I will be 65 in August so I've just about run my race here as well. I don't know what I'll do. I'm not sure what I'm going to do. It's a smashing wee pub. It's not the size of your living room. But it's your usual pub – football and racing. If you're ever up here, drop in.'

During his time at St James' Park, Jim scored some important goals and set two records that no one could beat: he was the scorer of the first European goal for the club and the first substitute to find the net. It seemed appropriate that the man who pulled defenders all over the pitch, went on to pull pints, although he might just have let Ron Guthrie pull his own pint.

Chapter 5

IRVING NATTRASS
(1970–79)

IRVING NATTRASS was born on 20 December 1952 in Fishburn, County Durham. A graduate of the junior structure, Irving signed professional with Newcastle United in July 1970 and went on to make 300 senior starts for the club, scoring a total of 22 goals. He also gained one England Under-23 cap. Like many professional footballers, the roots of Irving's career were to be found in his childhood.

'It's strange…it's just that I came from a mining town, a mining village really, and unlike the kids these days, all we had to play with basically was either a cricket bat and ball or a football. That was it. We used to spend hours in the back lane playing from eight, nine, ten years old, bouncing the footballs off the walls, driving the neighbours mad. From there, it was through school, playing football at school. I moved on to the grammar school at Ferryhill, played in the football team there. Then I was picked up, believe it or not, by a Newcastle scout by the name of Harry Nattrass, a lovely man but no relation. At the time, we had three or four county players in our school team. I never made it into the county team, but Harry came to me one day and said, "Look, I've got a couple of places left on our training for next season. What do you think?"

'Obviously it was Newcastle United that he was offering me. As a youngster I had always supported Newcastle as well as Manchester United, with the two fairly equally. They were the results that I used to look at first. The old Manchester United team had Bobby Charlton, George Best…and at Newcastle there was Wyn Davies, Bobby Moncur. From there, I used to train twice a week at Newcastle from the age of 14 to the age of 16. Basically it was the only thing I ever thought I wanted to do at that age. So, from the age of 14, I was going through to Newcastle. I mean, that was it, I was hooked line and sinker. It was a lot of hard work. I hardly missed a training session in two years.

'For me, it was getting home from school at five past four, rushing home, grabbing my kit, back on the bus at twenty past four, all the way through to Newcastle. I'd get into Newcastle for six o'clock, train until half past eight, then back on the bus or train, getting back home at half past 10 or 11 o'clock at night, twice a week. I played for the school at the weekend, on a Saturday morning. I would then whizz through to Newcastle to play for their junior team in the afternoon. I had no complaints; I just got on with it. It was just hard work and a little bit of luck, I have to say.

'I got offered an apprenticeship when I was 16. I grabbed it and after that it was just a case of "do your best" really. In our squad at the time I think that there were 12 of us. Three of them had played for England schoolboys, but none of them went on to make it. They were all released at 18 years old. But we had some good people. Keith Burkinshaw guided me through the early years and I have to say that he and Joe Harvey moulded me into the player that I became. Particularly Keith who spent many an afternoon, extra afternoons, with us, and I think that him first then Joe Harvey are the two main people I have to thank for what I achieved in football.'

Although Irving's first senior appearance was as a substitute against Derby County at St James' Park on 27 March 1971, his first full senior debut was away at Coventry City on 1 May 1971. He remembers it well.

'I actually joined the club as a centre-half/sweeper and I think the fact that I turned into a right-back was purely a coincidence. My first game at Newcastle was as a substitute against Derby County and John Craggs got injured. I went on into the right-back position, played half an hour at right-back, and had a stormer. It was from then that people thought "He's a right-back". But I always thought that centre-half was my best position.

'Coventry City away was my full debut. I remember it, playing alongside big John McNamee, as a kid really, and they had a centre-forward called Ernie Hunt who was giving me a bit of stick and a bit of physical aggravation. I'll never forget it to this day, the ball went out for a corner and John walked across to Ernie Hunt and he said, "Hey sonny, leave the kid alone." You just knew what John was like.'

Irving has visited the current St James' Park as a guest of honour on a number of occasions in more recent times and he recalled what it was like when he was playing there.

'My memory of the old stadium was the atmosphere, particularly when they had the Leazes End that was covered. I remember some great nights, full houses; the atmosphere was second to none. I don't think that they've actually been able to reproduce that same sort of atmosphere in the grounds and stands nowadays. It's very difficult. We used to get 45–50,000 people. Okay they were standing, but the atmosphere and the noise was just mind-boggling, it really was. It used to definitely give you a massive lift playing at home.

'I think we've come a long way since the Hillsborough disaster. There is certainly scope now to go back, not totally, but back to allowing those people who want stand in some areas to do so, certainly behind the goals. It would just create a much better atmosphere. I think this is why England have always struggled at Wembley. It's very difficult to create an atmosphere when the supporters are like 50 yards from the pitch.

'On match days, particularly home games, it was just a steady build-up. Joe Harvey had this aura about him. He didn't use to come into the dressing room until about 10 minutes before we went out. As soon as he walked in, the whole place lifted. Joe didn't use to say much other than, "Do the business, don't let the fans down, and don't let yourselves down. Let's get out there, do the business." Then he used to stand at the door with a bottle of whiskey. Those who wanted a quick swig were allowed a quick swig and a pat on the back. Joe would stand there and as you went past, it would be, "It's you or him", if you were given the job of marking somebody. He was down to earth. He was a fabulous man, a lovely man.

'I remember when I was negotiating a contract, I was getting £30 a week. I had just turned professional, been there a year, so I'd been offered a new contract, just broken into the first team, expected a good rise. I walked in to see Joe and said to him, "Joe, what's going on? You've offered me £40 a week. I'm not happy with that." He said, "Are you sure it's £40?" He knew that it was £40. Anyway, he picks up the phone and rings Russell Cushing and says, "Russell, you've made a mistake with this contract, it was £50 a week." Then he put the phone down and he said, "Are you happy with £50?" I said, "Oh yeah, I'm happy."

'Training, physically it was hard. I remember in pre-season my first week at Newcastle as a 16-year-old. It was mind-boggling in terms of how physically demanding it was. I look back now at some of the things we used to do. It was almost like being an Olympic athlete. But there was the whole team thing. When I went there, we had a team that had just won the Fairs Cup, with Pop Robson, Bobby Moncur, Frank Clark, all pros who would go out of their way to speak to you, to make you feel welcome, to help you. People don't realise the camaraderie you get with a bunch of players who have just won something and obviously want to go on and win more things. I don't suppose that the training has probably changed all that much. I think that the physical side of it has probably gone down a bit and obviously the development of more of the nutritional side of the game has come in. But I don't think it will be that much different.'

Ask any former footballer about his career and he will be able to recall some of the more memorable games that he played in. Some will be fond memories, others will not, especially when they involve losing to non-League opponents in the FA Cup.

'People still ask me now about Hereford and I say to them, it was one of those games, two games really, which were just fated. I remember vividly the home game when we were 2–0 up within a very short time, or so it seemed. We hit the post, hit the bar, it was bouncing along the goal-line. Before they scored, we should have been 6–0, 7–0 up. They gained two breaks, scored two goals. Then we pounded them again, hit the bar, there were people on the line. It was just one of those things, it was just meant to be. And it was the same down at Hereford really. It was the result that was obviously meant to be. We missed chances that Malcolm Macdonald had never missed before. What can you say? It was a growing up, I suppose. It makes you grow up very quickly. We went to Manchester United the week after and beat them 2–0 at Old Trafford. That's football.'

Irving missed out on the chance to play in the FA Cup final in 1974 through injury, the history of which went back to some earlier encounters with Birmingham City. It all started during a Texaco Cup game when Jimmy Smith was dismissed for a tackle that broke an opponent's leg.

'We had a bit of a pitch battle. I don't condone what Jimmy Smith did, but I can understand how it happened. Jimmy was a very skilful player, but he was also a hard player. He would never intentionally hurt anybody. The lad that he did hurt quite badly had actually done Tommy Gibb in the previous game, causing him to have a cartilage operation. He had gone over the top of Stewart Barrowclough in the same match, maybe five minutes before Jimmy tackled him. I remember that I was standing at the other end of the park and I heard the crack. Obviously Jimmy got sent off for that. I still don't condone what he did, but I can understand why he did it. I was just the unlucky one. Unfortunately we played them the following Saturday at Birmingham, and I was just the unlucky one really. To me the tackle on me was no worse than the one by Jimmy. I tore knee ligaments; he broke a leg. But the referee at Newcastle saw it; the referee at Birmingham didn't see it.

'What was even tougher about the Cup final was knowing that I probably could have played. I thought that I was fit enough to play. There was a surgeon at Newcastle General Hospital called Mr Todd who operated, fixed it, perfect. It was Mr Todd who insisted that I didn't play until the next season. But I was doing more than training by a month before the Cup final. I was 100 percent fit, raring to go, but the club kept holding me back. When I spoke to

Joe [Harvey], he said, "Well, I've got to do what the guy said." At the time he was struggling because David Craig had dislocated his elbow and it ended up with Frank Clark playing right-back and Alan Kennedy left-back. But it was tough. I didn't really want to go down for the final because it was really tough. Then I had Joe saying, "No, no, you're coming on the bus, you're coming to the hotel, and you're coming on the match bus with us." But it was tough.'

Irving did play in the League Cup final at Wembley in 1976, but this occasion was also tarnished by bad memories.

'My memory was that I bloody injured my knee again, my other knee, in the cup replay at Bolton. I didn't want to play this time and I said to Gordon Lee, "I'm not 100 percent, I'm struggling." He said, "Well, my feeling is that you've brought us this far, you go down, you go on the pitch, and if after two minutes you can't do it, you can come off. But I want you on the pitch at the start." I got through it, but looking back it was a bit unfair really on the team because I wasn't 100 percent fit. And we lost to a fluky goal. I thought that we were the better team on the day really.

'I still think that the best team performance I ever played in at Newcastle was when we beat Liverpool 4–1. They were European champions, I think top of the League, and we could have beaten them 10–1. I missed an open goal. From a team performance point of view, I remember Keith Burkinshaw saying at the team meeting the next morning, "That's the best team performance I have ever seen from any club in English football." Liverpool couldn't get the ball off us for five, six, seven minutes at a time. When I look back, without a doubt that's the best team performance. Highlight moments, you would think of your debut, playing at Wembley, playing for England in the Under-23s. I think all games at Newcastle were highlights, I really do.'

During my interview with Irving I reminded him that he scored 22 goals.

'I did, all good ones. There were two that stand out. One of them, I don't know if it was on *Match of the Day*, I think it was. It was against Wolves when Jimmy Smith played about a 60-yard ball across the pitch. I was on the halfway line, from the left-back position, and I went on and hit this ball from about 25 yards. It flew into the top corner with about 10 minutes to go. That was one and the other one was against Arsenal where we had a corner and the goalkeeper punched the ball out. It dropped from a great height about five yards outside the box, David Craig was just going to head it and I screamed at him to get out of the way. He sort of ducked and it was one of those things. I hit it and by the time I looked up it had hit the back of the net, in the top corner, and bounced out. So, it was coming back out and I thought that it had hit the bar until everybody turned away. Then I realised it had gone in. I think that was probably the best. I'm sure that the Tyne Tees television cameras were there for *Shoot*.

'The best goal I've ever seen was scored by Malcolm Macdonald against Leicester City. I remember that they were on the attack and whoever was in our goal caught the ball and threw it out to me, and I ran about 20 yards on a counter-attack. There was only Malcolm and I and I went to play a one-two with him. It must have been about 40 yards out. I flipped the ball to him and went for the return. He sort of let it run across him and I was just about to shout at him "You greedy…". Peter Shilton was in their goal and he never even moved. I have never seen a ball travel as quick. It just sort of flew into the top corner. I couldn't believe how quick it went. That was the best goal I think I have ever seen scored.

'Another great goal that I saw was scored by Tony Green. When I was 18, 19, I was playing as a holding midfield player and I had Tony Green just in front of me, I had Terry Hibbitt on the left, and I had Jimmy Smith on the right. It was like, get the ball, win the ball for them and then all I had to do was go and let them play. When they all played well, it was stunning. Tony Green was a fabulous player. It used to take Tony about 15 minutes to get into a game, and then he used to run it. During the first 15 minutes, you didn't see much of him, then after that he used to just run the game.

'The goal Tony scored was against Santos when Pele was playing and we played a friendly in Hong Kong. Tony scored a goal from about 35 yards out, putting it in the top corner. Playing against teams like that, the Brazilians, was a great experience. We came off the pitch after the game and quite a few of us had bruises around the ribs because as they were backing into you they were nipping you. They didn't just grab your shirt, they nipped you and pulled you as well.'

I personally moved to Newcastle as Malcolm Macdonald moved south to play for Arsenal. I asked Irving for his recollection of Supermac's impact at Newcastle United.

'Malcolm was pretty much an unknown to me when he came to Newcastle, other than I was aware that he had scored goals for Luton. I think that Malcolm was probably the best goalscorer, the best one-on-one finisher, I have ever seen, without a doubt. One-on-one with the goalkeeper, his percentage of scoring goals must have been very high. He very rarely missed when he got through. He was such a great goalscorer, with unbelievable pace. One thing that frightened defenders was the pace that people like Malcolm had. In today's football he would frighten people to death because of his pace and finishing.'

During Irving's playing career at St James' Park he encountered a number of different managers. He agreed to share his thoughts on the various changes that he experienced.

'In my opinion they dropped a mega mistake because the successor to Joe Harvey should have been Keith Burkinshaw. His record speaks for itself. Whether it was political or not, I don't know, but the natural successor should have been Keith. I think if that had happened, he would have been at the club for a number of years, without a doubt. Gordon Lee came in and I thought he was good at getting the best out of players. Mind you, he also made a mega mistake selling Malcolm [Macdonald]. Having structured the team, to the team that he wanted, Gordon made his decision to leave, which was inexcusable, it really was.

'Then we all got carried along with the Richard Dinnis thing. Richard did well, he had the benefit of following Gordon Lee, because we had a fabulous team spirit. We finished fifth in the First Division and we had a great team spirit. But then it fell apart. Richard was basically wanting the players to hold it together when it should have been the manager holding it together the following season. When things went wrong, then he didn't really know the answers to put them right. But I still think that Keith Burkinshaw should have taken over from Joe. Richard Dinnis let us all down by moving at a time when he had made crucial decisions to get rid of certain players and then he left, which I think was wrong.

'I remember when I moved to Middlesbrough and I came back to play at Newcastle, what a fabulous reception I got from the fans and it made me realise what I should have done. Bill McGarry was manager at Newcastle when I left. He was a horrible man. Had I hung on for six months, I would have realised that with him as manager, there was only one way Newcastle were going to go. They were never going to be successful with him as manager. It would only have been a matter of time before he would have gone and I should have hung on really. I should have hung on and stayed. But hindsight is a great thing.'

It was inevitable that we would talk about playing football on today's pitches and also the infamous slope at St James' Park.

'I think the way football is played now would suit me. I was never a physical player. I played 300 and odd games for Newcastle United and 200 games for Middlesbrough. I got booked twice or maybe three times and I was never sent off. I didn't get booked for fouls; it was more like for throwing the ball away. I do think that football today would suit me. I think the training would also suit me. I think that I would really enjoy playing football today.

'If you were sitting in the dugout you could see half the play on the right wing. When you were on the pitch that wasn't the case, everything was alright. I think we played Tottenham in the second leg of the League Cup semi-final and they beat us 1–0 at Tottenham. The second game was at Newcastle. You always had the wind blowing from the Leazes down to the Gallowgate. There was a slight slope, very slight, but there was a definite slope. Before we even started the thinking was, with the strong wind and the slope, if we win the toss, we'll kick up the slope. If we are 0–0 at half-time, that would suit us fine. Then we won the toss, kicked up the slope, and scored a goal in the first two minutes. We then basically just sat on it, going in at half-time 1–0 up. In the second half, playing down the slope, we always liked to play it that way.

'Teams used to know this. I remember when we played against Everton; I was captain at the time. I remember losing the toss and there was quite a breeze blowing down the pitch. The other captain, having won the toss, decided to play with the wind in the first half, down the slope. I thought "great". I think we scored three goals up the slope in the first half.

'The playing surfaces now are so much better. We played on some horrendous pitches. They wouldn't even inspect those pitches these days. I remember when we played a cup-tie at Walsall on a pitch where you had to flick the ball up and volley it rather than try and pass it. That was a game that would never be played these days. You could play on pitches now at the end of the season and they are like bowling greens. Mind you, the stands nowadays are blocking out natural sunlight and you are going to struggle.'

When the interview inevitably turned to the area of humorous stories, Irving selected a couple of gems involving a manager and the club surgeon.

'I'll tell you one about Bill McGarry. This just about sums the guy up. He used to have this thing about the old guys against the young lads when we were playing five-a-side. We went on a pre-season trip to Jersey, a training trip, so the first day we were there it was five-a-side. McGarry says, "Right, five-a-side in this park. Grab this park bench, grab that park bench, five-a-side pitch, two park benches. You old guys over there, young kids over there. The young kids will wallop you all day long." Of course they never used to.

'So, this first day, we beat the kids whatever. The next day, we'd do the physical side, finish off, five-a-side. He would say, "Old guys over there, same teams as yesterday, young lads over there. I'll sort you out today. I'm going to make the pitch bigger." There were only 16 of us, so it was like eight-a-side. So he moves the benches and it's probably the size of a full football pitch on a park. We beat the young lads again. So the next day it was, "Old guys over there, young lads over there. I'll sort you out today; grab that bench. Aye, the young lads will run you ragged." It was like two football pitches long. We beat them again.

'So on the final day, he says to the young lads, "Right, if you don't beat them today, you'll be running round this park all afternoon." This pitch was now like two and a half football pitches long and two and a half football pitches wide, honestly. There were 16 of us playing. So we were beating the young lads again and they're trying to score, and there's Bill McGarry with this park bench on his shoulders walking down the park. By the time he'd finished, he'd got to the other end of the park and he must have been about six football pitches away. We could barely see him in the distance. He puts the bench down and that was it, we just couldn't do anything but laugh. I still remember that. He had these young lads in the park all afternoon running around.

'We were playing this game against Birmingham, nothing related to the injury, and I remember heading the ball and all of a sudden I was just seeing stars, basically just being stunned for two or three seconds. My eye wasn't bleeding at all. Pat Howard came across and he said, "God, you've got a nasty one, stay there, stay down, you've got a nasty one." Keith Burkinshaw, who was the trainer, came on and said, "You've got a nasty one; you'll have to come off." So I came off the pitch and the doc looked at me and said, "I can't do that, you'll have to go to hospital."

'Then one of the directors, Fenton Braithwaite, came in – a lovely guy, used to be a plastic surgeon. He was 70 years old and he was ******. He was always at the matches. This was like 10 minutes from the end. He used to wear these low-rimmed spectacles. He came, swaying, and he said this and that to the doctor, and I'm thinking. "What's he going to do?" Then he puts these gloves on and he's got a napkin tucked in. He always wore these old fancy waistcoats. So he's got the waistcoat on, sleeves rolled up, and he picks up a needle. He says, "You'll only feel four or five pricks, but a big lad like you, you'll not notice it." Then I looked and I thought, "He's not going to stick that needle in my eye?"

'He never flinched at all. I had 19 stitches in my eye, in the muscle, I had about 12 in the inside, and about nine on the side, and I never felt a thing; Within about three or four weeks there wasn't a mark on it. I just couldn't believe it. I went to see him with a bottle of whiskey to thank him. But it was so funny, everybody stood there laughing. The doc used to stitch everybody. He was one of those people who would rush in and get you back on the pitch. When he saw me, he just said, "I can't do that."

'There were some colourful characters on the board. Everybody used to really say nasty things about the board, but we really had some good characters. Unfortunately the people with the power were the ones who ruled the place. Then we had Fenton Braithwaite who was a lovely man, we had Jimmy Rush who used to be a fighter pilot in the war, and we had three or four really nice people who really wanted the club to succeed and would have done anything. But you've got the other ones, the Lord Westwoods, who were really in it for the money or themselves.'

Irving left Newcastle United in July 1979 having been transferred to Middlesbrough for £375,000, allowing him to move back into the old First Division. He later retired from professional football in 1986 due to injury. Looking back, Irving's career blossomed courtesy of a knowledgeable man sharing the same surname, a lot of hard work and a little bit of luck. Of course, he was also helped by players being encouraged to 'leave the kid alone'.

Chapter 6

TONY GREEN
(1971–73)

ANTHONY GREEN was born on 30 October 1946 in Kinning Park, Glasgow. Signed from Blackpool in October 1971 in a deal that saw Keith Dyson travel in the opposite direction, Tony only made 38 senior starts for Newcastle United due to being forced to retire early through injury. He scored three goals for Newcastle and gained six full caps playing for Scotland.

The seeds of Tony's football career were sown early in his childhood when he followed the family trend.

'When I look back, I had two older brothers, and we moved to one of these big housing estates in Glasgow. I was eight years old at the time. My two older brothers, they were into football and I think that I just followed everything that they did. In those days there was no other sport, so you just played street teams, one against the other, every morning, noon and night when you were a kid, from the age of eight until when we left home. All we did was play football.'

Living in Glasgow as a child, I did wonder how Tony had chosen which Old Firm team to support.

'Well again through my brothers, my oldest brother is still a Celtic fanatic. So when we were brought up, we lived on this big housing estate where half of the kids supported Rangers and the other half supported Celtic. So I was just brought up supporting Celtic. I would probably have ended up supporting Celtic anyway, but you've got a head start when you've got older brothers, in lots of things, don't you?'

After a period of playing football in his native Scotland, Tony's professional career was to take off in a sudden and unexpected way, seeing him move south of the border.

'I stayed on at school until I was 18, so I played like junior football. I don't know if they had that in England. There used to be a step between juvenile and professional, it was junior. So I had a year there, then I played for Albion Rovers for two years. Then I went to Blackpool in 1967. In actual fact, what actually happened was we had an early kick-off because Celtic were playing a cup final in 1967. I think that they had already won the European Cup. So there was a cup final and we had tickets. They played a lot of matches with an 11 o'clock kick-off to let people go to the football. I went to the match, then I went to my girlfriend's house after it had finished.

'Stan Mortensen and Harry Johnson were there and I ended up signing for Blackpool. There was a reporter who used to write in the *Express*, he stopped my dad in the street. We lived about maybe five miles away from my girlfriend's house and he just asked my dad where I lived. He said, "I'm his father", and the reporter said, "Well, he's signing for Blackpool". My dad said, "Well, he doesn't know anything about it because he's at the football match." So my dad jumped in the car and went to my girlfriend's house. When I got there, there was Stan Mortensen, Harry Johnson and my dad all waiting for me.

'When I first went to Blackpool there were a lot of clubs interested initially, and then I bust my Achilles tendon. Then, when I came back, Bob Stokoe became manager. There were a few clubs interested. Leeds were interested and they got in touch with me and told me not to sign for anyone else. But I didn't know then, I just found out a few years ago, that Bob Stokoe absolutely hated Don Revie. When Don Revie came to the house to try and get information, Bob never let him over the doorstep. He actually kept him at the door. Bob was desperate for me to go anywhere else but Leeds. It couldn't happen nowadays. Then Joe Harvey came in and I think Bob wanted me to go to Newcastle. Joe came in, we met and just agreed terms. So that was it.'

Tony made his debut for Newcastle United away against Everton on 30 October 1971 on his birthday. I asked him about his early memories of the move to St James' Park, training and match-day routines.

'My debut, away at Everton, it was on my 25th birthday. I can remember that it just seemed to be a completely different game at home and away. At Blackpool, you didn't get the support that Newcastle had, so I think that I was quite overcome. I was quite surprised at the support because I had never even seen a match at Newcastle. I was quite surprised at the fervour of the whole place and it has never left me to this day. I still get gobsmacked.

'The stadium was completely different to what it is now, obviously. What actually happened, when I went to Newcastle, they were knocking down the old [East] stand to build a new one, so there were no supporters on that side. I think that the average attendance was something like 36,000. Even with no supporters on one side, the rest just seemed to make as much noise. So it made no difference. My biggest memory is the first day – it was freezing. Even coming from Glasgow and living in the north, I didn't realise that it was so cold. I couldn't understand it. I can remember it in the changing room with people putting on woollies and bobble hats and all sorts, and I thought, "I can't understand this". But I could once we got to the training ground at Benwell; it was so cold.

'I lived in Dinnington, near Newcastle. There was nothing really different on match days, I was maybe a bit nervous. You would just go in and get there. In fact, I don't think that I drove there, to be honest, because I was never interested in cars. So I think my wife would take me in or I would get a lift with somebody. I was at Dinnington, so it was only a quarter of an hour into Newcastle. You would just get there at two o'clock and you would get the buzz. For home matches, you would have a steak at 12 o'clock, which I think was probably the worst thing that could happen. For away matches, you had to leave on the Friday; I don't know if it is still the same. We used to stop on the way, just before you reached the M6, and we would have tea, scones and cakes, which again I didn't think was the best thing to do either.'

For the Newcastle United supporters who were fortunate to have seen Tony play, there are likely to have been many memorable performances. Tony recalled some of them.

'The one game that is remembered the most is after the

Hereford defeat in the FA Cup when we beat Manchester United. That was the only time we'd ever beaten Man United at Old Trafford in 30 years or something. For me that is the one that Newcastle supporters want to talk to me about. I can still remember the week after, we played Everton at home and there were over 30,000 there. We played them off the pitch. We hit the bar and we still couldn't score. The Hereford game came in the middle of a really good run. It just happened.

'One of my favourite stories is this one. It is one of the best. It was probably about 10 years ago. Roger Hunt, who played for Liverpool, said to me, "I've got a pal who is dying to meet you, he is a big Newcastle supporter. He's got a pub, so we'll go and see him." So we went to see this fella and he is talking about the time we played Liverpool at Anfield. He is telling Roger that we played them off the pitch, telling him that I was in a different class to Kevin Keegan, saying the only difference was that Ray Clemence had a great game, and we basically played them off the pitch. Roger said, "What was the score?" His pal says, "Oh, Liverpool won 5-0." I tell you, he wasn't trying to be clever. We still talk about that. It was just so matter of fact the way he said we were a different class to Liverpool. That shows what it means to be a true Newcastle supporter. Also, that was probably the only time that we lost by more than one goal the full season that I played.'

Tony gained six full international caps playing for his country, but sadly his injury put an end to a career of huge potential. Tony recalled his all-too-brief experience of international football.

'Actually, I think that I came on as a sub a couple of times before I got a full game. I think that there was one of those games where the team was getting slaughtered and you come on as sub and you just get swamped by the whole situation. I think that I came on as a sub against Belgium and against Holland, when it was really backs-to-the-wall stuff. My first full cap, I think I played against Ireland at Hampden. Then I played against England at Wembley.'

Tony Green was a truly gifted player and this was recognised by the fact that he was named Player of the Year, and won the Man of the Match award so many times as reported in the local paper, during his short career with Newcastle United. Although Tony was sort of aware of the awards, it was several years later that he found out just how many times he had achieved them.

'I don't know what they do now, if they still do it, but what they used to do was to ask the opposition manager who he thought was Newcastle's best player. I think they would ask the opposition manager or maybe the captain who was the best player. By the end of the season, I think I had maybe played 30-odd games and I had got about 25 Man of the Match awards, something like that.

'My dad died about a year ago and I found a suitcase. I don't know where he got them from, but there were a lot of cuttings of the Man of the Match pieces from the local Monday paper. I hadn't even seen them before. Well, maybe I had seen them but never taken much notice of them. But I found about a dozen of them that he must have cut out of the paper lying at the bottom of the suitcase. Maybe he had been in Newcastle when it was in the *Evening Chronicle* on a Monday. They were just a couple of inches with what the opposition manager had said. There was like a League table. They would say that I had so many, Malcolm Macdonald had so many, Bobby Moncur had so many, and then they would tally them up at the end of the season.'

Tony became an instant idol on his arrival on Tyneside and the admiration was mutual from the start, continuing to this day.

'I loved playing there more than anywhere. Even now I still support Newcastle. The club wasn't the best-run club. It was a disaster in many ways, but the supporters made up for it. I'm not sure what goes on now, but even now the supporters are still the same. I was out on Friday night in Blackpool and someone came up to ask us to have my picture taken. He said, "You were my father's favourite player." Sometimes now I get people saying, "You

were my granddad's favourite player." But it happens quite a lot and it is nice.'

As a footballer Tony was destined for greatness. Everyone who saw him play could only marvel at his skills on the ball. Sadly it all came to an abrupt end on 2 September 1972 when a heavy tackle by a Crystal Palace defender caused an injury that would ultimately seal his fate. It was an injury that effectively ended his career.

'What actually happened, I think that I lost the ball and I chased it. Well you know when you try to tackle, which was not my strongest point, I sort of put my foot in and I got knocked off balance, and my knee just went. Then there was a bit of a mix up with the whole thing because the medical care at Newcastle wasn't the best at that time. After three months I asked to be sent to Wigan to see the specialist who had treated me at Blackpool. But then when I came back, after I played, my knee used to blow up.

'I don't know if it was arthritis or what it was, but I played in the reserves at Coventry and I think that we won 1–0 and I scored, and my knee was great. Tommy Hutchinson, who had been at Blackpool with me, played for Coventry and he came to see me after the game. We had a few beers and I was really feeling on top of the world. The next morning my knee, I just couldn't move it. I realised that when I had rested it after I had played, it would just come up like a balloon. I eventually had to keep getting the fluid taken out of it because it just kept blowing up after I had played.'

On Friday 10 May 1974, Tony Green was given a testimonial against Middlesbrough. In the match programme, manager Joe Harvey said, 'Tony Green was one of my best buys…I could watch Tony play all day…we have never been able to replace him. It's hard to replace a genius. It was one of the saddest moments of my career as a manager when Tony came to see me one Sunday morning and told me that he would never play again…he was almost in tears.' Tony recalled that moment.

Chapter 6: TONY GREEN

'It was a nice thing to say. In fact, I think I had to reassure Joe, you know. When I went in to see him, I think that he was more upset than I was. I was saying, "It's okay, Joe". To be honest, I think that the testimonial said more for the Newcastle supporters. I don't honestly think there has been anybody who has played for such a short time who has had so much adulation as I have. I don't think that there has been anybody, really.

'As soon as I finished playing, they just said if I wanted a testimonial, I could have one at the end of the season. It was a funny sort of thing because Newcastle had a match on the Saturday. So I just sort of thought that Joe would have to play the reserves. So I went to see Joe during the week and I said, "There is a League match on the Saturday and I've got a testimonial on the Friday." Joe said to me, "Look, there will be hundreds of League matches after this, but you are only going to have one testimonial. You get to pick the best players and I will sort out what we have got left on the Saturday."

'It was an incredibly nice thing to do. He just told me to pick whoever I wanted. In those days there were home internationals and things like that, so there were a few players involved in those. But Joe was more interested in the testimonial than he was in the League game.

'At that time there were loads of people, like the doormen, who all came up and gave me their wages. They were saying things like, "It's been nice watching you play. Will you take my wages?" I finished up with all these wage packets. I kept them but sometimes I ended up breaking into them. It's funny, but I do regret that because I would like to have seen their names. There was quite a big crowd at the match and there was a director, Fenton Braithwaite, who said to me "I want a word with you". Then he gave me something and he said, "You have all your family here, you are going to be entertaining all night. You don't want to be spending all your own money." He gave me something like £30 or

£40. Loads of things like that happened. I look back and it was incredibly nice.'

Although the way Tony's playing career ended brought much sadness to Tyneside, he had some good times as well.

'I remember little things like when we played Wolves once and they beat us, and I argued with Terry Hibbitt after the game. A few other players got involved, they were like having a go at Terry. So, while the place is in uproar, Terry says to me, "Have you met my brother?" I said no and he says, "Come and meet him". So, we left the dressing room and there's all hell let loose. Then there's me and Terry, who's started it, we were in the bar drinking with his brother while everybody else is left hacking away at each other. He was like that was Terry. He could cause a row in an empty house.'

Since retiring from playing football, Tony has been kept busy acting as a member of the Pools Panel – that invisible body of people who decide the results of postponed matches on a Saturday. Until recently, Tony was one of two former Newcastle United players who were on the panel.

'Not long ago Ronnie Simpson died, so there's just Roger Hunt, Gordon Banks and myself now. So, it must be nearly 29 or 30 years that I have done. You just go to form or try to work out what the results would have been. You get matches like Liverpool at home or Manchester United away, and you can get all different opinions. You just have to argue it out until you can agree. I have really enjoyed it.'

In his testimonial programme notes Tony said, 'This strange game of football has nothing but happy memories for me, and the happiest of all are here at St James' Park. I've always done my best to entertain the fans and I've always been most appreciative of the support they've given me.' To this day Tony still follows the fortunes of Newcastle United.

'The nice thing is that the manager of my local pub is a Newcastle fanatic, so if Newcastle are on the telly, he's got a hard core of about eight people that come in with their black and white scarves on. Of course, if Manchester United are on the telly, there are about a hundred of them who come in. But if Newcastle are on the telly, I'll go to the pub and watch the match.'

I asked Tony if he would have enjoyed gracing the current St James' Park pitch.

'I would love to play now, but you can't have any regrets. What's happened, you cannot change your age, can you? I think at the top the standard is terrific, but I think near the bottom it's worse than it used to be. I think that people at the top like Shearer and Henry are sensational. They keep getting better than the people were in my era. It is a lot more professional now. If you are going to be a professional footballer and you can pick your time, this is the time to play, isn't it? I loved it, but that's life.'

During my interview with Tony, what shone throughout was what a real gentleman he is. There was not a hint of bitterness at the way his football career ended. Tony's dream was to play for Newcastle United in the FA Cup final at Wembley. When Newcastle United played in the FA Cup final in 1974, Tony could only watch the game as a supporter. If Tony had been playing for Newcastle with the vastly improved medical care that is available today, his career might well have been saved and he might just have received an FA Cup winners' medal.

To those supporters who saw Tony Green play for Newcastle United, he was a genius, and to his manager he was a genius. When Tony first arrived on Tyneside, he could not believe how cold it was. Now, whenever he visits the city, Tony still cannot believe how warm the welcome always is.

Chapter 7

JOHN TUDOR
(1971–76)

JOHN TUDOR was born on 24 June 1946 in Ilkeston, Derbyshire. He was transferred to Newcastle United from Sheffield United in January 1971 and, playing as a striker, he went on to make 216 senior starts for the club and scored 73 goals. The foundations of John's football destiny were very much laid as a child in the family home.

'Well, like every kid, I think that you are just born into it when you are in a football family. That was the number one thing. My dad and all his brothers played. My dad briefly went to Leicester City as a trialist a lot of years ago. I think that he was actually offered some form of contract there because he was one of the local home-grown players in the Ilkeston, Derbyshire, area where I'm from. He evolved to score a lot of goals. He was a small, stocky type of centre-forward who scored a lot of goals. He was offered a contract at Leicester but I think that there were problems at home. He needed the money because he was a builder in a building company. Then he wanted to leave due to the problems at home, stuff like that. I don't really know but that's the story I picked up.

'My dad and his brother, Albert, were both very good players who played together in the same pit team. So, when you're surrounded by that, plus the fact that there wasn't a great deal else you wanted to do at night but play football. You just pick up games every weekend and then you get to an age where you start to put your name on the map. You start in local football, starting to score goals, and then people want you to come and sign for them. So I went to a number of youth squads. My first recollection of anything that was out of the ordinary was to play for the Ilkeston and District XI. Would you believe, we played in black and white stripes; shirts donated by Notts County at that time. I played in a few of their district games and became a county player. Then, I would be about 12, 13, 14, and I just sort of migrated into local football, playing for various street teams and local village teams. I made my mark in a place called Stanley Common, which is near Derby, in between Derby and Ilkeston, where we lived. It was a little village where they had a very up and coming, very adventurous club. I got into them, to play one or two games. One name that stands out, a guy called Peter Daniels, who used to play for Derby when Cloughie was there, was a full-back. He played for the same team as I did and he went on to Derby.

Chapter 7: JOHN TUDOR

'I left school, went down the pit, went to Sheffield United, played a couple of games over a couple of weekends. I went to Chesterfield, to Middlesbrough, to Forest, to Notts County, to Derby County, just playing various games for them, filling in more than anything else. Nobody really came to say this is what you need to do or we need to sign you up. Apart from Forest and Derby where I was constantly, I had a long time at Middlesbrough. I travelled up there for the best part of three quarters of a season, over a year, coming up to Middlesbrough every weekend to play for them. I played in the reserves as well. And I thought I was going to get something there. Raich Carter was manager then, it goes back a long time. I think that he got fired or something and I never heard from them again. It was as simple as that, here today gone tomorrow. One day you get a card through the post, the next day you're not getting anything. I don't know what happened.

'But I was doing alright. I got as far as the reserve team. I got into the Midland League with a guy called Jim Raynor who played for Peterborough, and he was the manager of Ilkeston Town. I got into the reserve team and played a few times, then I got into the first team. And that is basically where it all started.'

Before becoming a professional footballer John had a variety of jobs and he recalled that life was not always easy.

'Oh yeah, I did everything; everything and nothing. As I say, I came out of school on the Friday and I was down the pit on the Monday as an apprentice electrician. I didn't like it of course; I hated it. My dad was down the same pit, he was a deputy down the same pit, so I had to do what he told me to do. I was down there about six, seven or eight weeks, then I just quit; I didn't like it. I just said, "No, I'm not going down there again." I started on a building site, had about five or six jobs over a space of three to four years where I just piddled about at anything that paid me a bit of money.

'Then right out of the blue, when I was playing for Ilkeston Town, Jim Raynor played in a charity game, playing against a select team from Coventry City, and Jimmy Hill was playing. Their youth development officer also played. Jim just happened to mention young kids and he arranged to send myself and Brian Wright, a full-back who had come through at the same time as I had. Unfortunately for Brian, he didn't show, so I went off on my own to Coventry. They gave me a month – two weeks before Christmas and two weeks in the New Year – to prove that I could play. There was no danger I couldn't play. I mean, I wasn't a player as such like they are today, but I could make things happen if I got the right sort of service. Consequently I went in there, played in the youth team. I'd been playing men's football for about 18 months. So I went in there and it was relatively easy to get on the end of things because you were playing with players who were good. It wasn't long before I was slamming balls in the back of the net on a regular basis.

'I got straight into all the training facilities, the extras that were on hand in that two weeks, showed a tremendous interest and a tremendous work ethic. They sent me home for Christmas with a bag of stuff: turkey in a bag, nuts, crisps and stuff. When I came back after Christmas, then they said, "We'd like you to stay, give you a six months contract 'til the end of the year, see how you go." They also found out I was too old to play for the youth cup team and they really wanted someone who could play for that team. So unfortunately that was a bit of a back step, but they decided to keep me on anyway. I think it was a toss-up between two or three people, flipping coins in the changing room. I think they had 58 pros then at Coventry. To keep big squads, I think they were only on £20 a week, so it didn't really matter. So I decided to stay until the end of the year, I signed a six months contract, then worked my socks off, I really worked hard. That's basically how it all started.'

Taking him back to his childhood again, I asked John about his football heroes when he was growing up in Derbyshire.

Chapter 7: JOHN TUDOR

'I don't think I really had any. My hero was my dad. I wanted to do what my dad did, which was to score goals readily. He was only a small fella, but he got in the right gaps to score goals between people. He was tough. I suppose I didn't really follow football apart from Derby, Forest, Notts County. I got a sort of hankering towards Notts County, but then it was more to play all the time. I wasn't the sort of person to pick a newspaper up and see the stuff that's in there today. The media's different now, stuff like that. That's the thing that's generated all this stuff in the papers today. But when I played, we didn't even have a telly. I can remember the day that the telly arrived and it was placed proudly on my mother's sewing machine, sitting by the window. Then a new life started.

'I can remember my Uncle Albert, who was my dad's brother, he was probably the better player. I can remember him once taking me to Stoke City, the Victoria Ground, to watch Stanley Matthews and I was only tiny. I didn't see much of Stanley Matthews because I was right down at the front at the wall. I probably just saw a pair of legs, but I saw legs all night. So I don't know what I went for, I didn't see it as a spectacle in the stand you were in, I was just on the terracing. I remember we were near the dugout. Years later I actually went to Stoke and I remembered where I'd stood. I actually went to a local journalist and said, "I stood there when I was like seven".'

John signed for Newcastle United in January 1971 when he was with Sheffield United. I asked him about the developments leading to his move.

'I'd heard a rumbling. There were one or two little pieces in the local press or in the national press. The *News of the World on Sunday* would have "Sheffield United striker John Tudor is in line to join this club or that club". There were two or three clubs interested just like there was when I left Coventry. There was a lot of speculation that I was going to leave. Sunderland wanted me apparently at one time. And it was like, "Are you going to let me go or let me know what's going on?" They would say, "Oh no, we're not going to sell you. You'd be the last person that's going to go. We're going to keep the kids because we've got no money." It looked like they were going to get relegated again but they didn't. They were in and out, on the brink all the time. Then right out of the blue we were suddenly at, "Right, you can go, £65,000, Sheffield United". And then, ****** me, about two and a half years later exactly the same thing happened again. There was like all this speculation but nothing concrete. I was at Lilleshall with Sheffield United; we'd gone there for the week to do in-depth training. I'd just teed off on the first tee, we were playing golf, and John Short, who was the first-team coach, came up to me and said, "Put your stuff away, you're going home. We need you back at the ground. There's a guy coming to talk to you."

'All the way home, all the way back to Sheffield, nobody talked to me. There were three guys in the car and nobody spoke to me. I was saying, "What's happening?" The reply was just "Oh, you're just going to meet somebody." They wouldn't say who it was. We got to the ground and they said, "Oh, he's not here, he's not arrived yet. You need to go home." So I went home, I just drove home. I spoke to my wife because I had to be back at the ground by 7.30 at night. I got back, sat waiting around for an hour, then Joe Harvey came in. He just started telling me how fantastic Newcastle was. It was, "Ever heard of this guy, ever heard of that guy, ever been to the North East?" I'd never really been to the North East, never been up there, never played up there. I played against Newcastle, Sunderland and Middlesbrough. I'd never been further north than Middlesbrough. I used to think, where is this place? Anyway, he kept telling me about Pop Robson, kept telling me about Wyn Davies, and I'm thinking, "How the hell am I going to get into a team like this?" And he told me that they'd just recently won the Fairs Cup, they were rebuilding, this that and the other, this is what is going to happen. I said, "Well, okay."

'I'll tell you what had happened. When I first got a glimpse of Newcastle, we'd played against them at Bramall Lane in the FA Cup, I think it was, or the League Cup, and we beat them 2–1 and I scored both goals. I scored with a header from a corner and Joe kept going on about that, my aerial presence, my strength in the air. But then he'd got Wyn Davies there as well. I didn't know what Wyn was like because he didn't score goals; he was just good in the air. It wasn't until we got into training that I realised what a tremendous presence he was. And I thought, sorry, no end result here. But I didn't know that he was hopefully going to bring Mal [Malcolm Macdonald] in. I went in the January, he bought Terry [McDermott] in about February/March time, and then he brought Mal in for the start of the season. So he was planning big things and I know that he'd been looking at McDermott for a long time, when he bought him as well.'

When John moved to Newcastle United in January 1971, it was winter of course and perhaps not the best time to arrive in the area. John remembered it well.

'I remember my first day like it was yesterday. I walked down the tunnel and I was told that there was going to be a picture shoot. It was windy, it was blowing a bloody gale actually, it was freezing cold, it was a dark dingy day. You could say it was typical. I walked onto the field and it was like a cowpat. It was the worst field – I'd been on better fields in my local backyard. It was awful; it was absolutely crap. It was rock hard, there was hardly any grass on it, and there were two or three fellas on there, walking up and down picking divots up and throwing them onto the track or putting them in a bucket and emptying them onto the track. And I thought, "****, I've never seen this before." I also thought, "God, what an awful place to play." I thought, "How on earth can you keep the ball on the ground?" It was just a tip, a total tip. Like I say, I wasn't the best player in the world, but give me these fields they play on today and I think I could do something with them. Where we are at the moment in the US, our climate is like 110 degrees red-hot, you can't breathe in the summer, and it's 70 degrees below in the winter. So we have these big domes built and we have plastic grass laid down. This new plastic grass is phenomenal. It'll not be long before it starts coming big time over in the UK. It's got to; it's super stuff.

'For the rest of my first week I stayed in the County Hotel, down by the railway station, and it ****** it down with rain all week. It just rained and rained and rained. I think I came up on a Monday and I stayed all week. Then I went home to Sheffield on the Friday night and I was told to meet the team on the Saturday in Burnley. So I went home to Sheffield and then travelled to Burnley on the Saturday in a car. I loaded my wife and a couple of friends into the car and we went to the game. I joined the team in a hotel, met the guys, we had lunch and stuff, trained again and went through some tactical stuff. And I couldn't see myself where I was going to fit in because they sort of talked round me. And it was like, hey where am I going to play? They said, "Well, we want to play three forwards today and you'll be the third forward. You play with Wyn up front and Pop will get everything flicked off him." In the game everything was in the air. I don't know what the score was but it was all Burnley. It was alright actually.'

Having shared his thoughts about his introduction to the pitch at St James' Park, I wondered if John's memories of training were any better.

'Training was either up at Hunters Moor or another place down by the river, and that was all red mud where the iron works were. So we used to come home all caked in red mud. That was just awash with water. That was about it, and then there was the car park, that was crap. I remember coming in on the first day and trying to get into some training equipment. Guys walked in with baskets of training gear and it was like, dive in and get what you could. But it had been the same at Sheffield. I remember Tony Green coming up and signing. He came in on the first day and it was one of those typical bleak days. We'd met him in the changing room and he was being interviewed by various people. Then we walked up to Hunters Moor to train and it was absolutely bitter. It was so cold that the ground was rock hard. By the time Tony got to the kitbag there was nothing left. So he'd got a little t-shirt on, an old rugby shirt ripped up to shreds, odd socks, raggy shorts and nothing else. Inside 20 minutes he was blue. I always remember that because I felt so sorry for him. I had been there myself.'

John's first experience of playing at St James' Park did little to improve his first impression of Newcastle United. He recalled that particular day and match days in general.

'We played at Burnley, then I think the first home game was Chelsea. I think they beat us 1–0 and it was appalling. The field was crap, oh god it was awful. We just couldn't play, you couldn't play on it, so we played over the top of it. We just swiped it then ran after it. It was no wonder Jinky [Jimmy Smith] couldn't get in the team. But he was suspended when I came. I think that Jinky had been a bit naughty and he'd been demoted to the reserves. On match days I used to tape my ankles, stuff like that. We used to have these red plastic canisters with the white tape inside. I'd get my ankles done, put on my socks, jockstrap and boots, hang around 'til the last couple of minutes, then put on my shirt and shorts. When Mal arrived, I'd go into the bathrooms and get some water in a glass and leave it by his side. He used to put his teeth in there. Some days were horrific. You'd be going out at five to three, the bell would be ringing, you'd go out there and it would be really bleak. You would warm up in the bath and, on cold days, Mutchie used to be standing there with a bottle of whiskey. You'd swill your mouth out or take a breath and swallow it. I remember seeing Willie McFaul doing that one day and he must have taken a bit too much because he puked in the tunnel.'

When John moved to St James' Park, he found the style of play a little different to what he had been used to at his previous clubs.

Consequently it took him a while to adjust to things and to convince the supporters that he would be successful.

'I suppose I was fortunate at Sheffield United. I had Alan Woodward, a full England international right-winger and Gill Reece, a full Welsh international left-winger, and they could both cross footballs like nobody's business. So it was dead easy. Remember I was only the end product. I was something that a guy called Arthur Reilly brought to Sheffield United. I was playing at the back of Maurice Setters at Coventry at the time. I was a centre-back and I played there for the biggest part of the whole season. Then Arthur came and bought me and he said, "I want you to go and play up front." I said, "I've not played up front for a season." He said, "I've got just the place for you. Go and stand in the six-yard box, just like that, and I'll get the ball to you." I had Tony Currie playing in behind me as a third striker, so it was easy. Nobody could live with Woodward. He was lightning fast, he could cross a ball on the run, and he could cross a ball standing still. He could ping it, he could curl it, he could loft them, and Reece was the same. So it was easy, I just went and stood in the six-yard box and got in the way. I played against Bury in the first game and I never got a kick for 40 minutes. Then I scored two goals in two minutes, standing in the six-yard box getting in the way. The 'keeper stopped one point blank and it dropped and I knocked it in. Then I got on the end of a cross. Getting on the end of the crosses was never a problem to me. I could do it when I was a kid.

'So I came to Newcastle and there were no flank players. Everything was long and then the flick on, long and flick on. So it wasn't until Hibby [Terry Hibbitt] came that it changed. It took him a long time to get into it, he was always playing behind and hitting it long. We never really got anybody out wide. I think at the time he'd got Barrowclough in the team, but he was only like 17 or 18, so he was still working with him, trying to get him going. But we had no flank players so it was a waste of time. You couldn't ask me to do what Mal could do. I could hold it up a little bit, bring people in, but get past people, dribble past people, forget it. That wasn't the point of my being there; I was the end product. Wherever I've been, I had service, people getting balls into the box, and I'd get on the end of them. That was it; that was the difference. I could compete in midfield, jumping and heading, I could compete physically and work hard. That's never been a problem. The gloss, little flicks, little touches, one-touch passes, not a problem, but the glitz and the glamour and the lightning pace that Mal had, stuff like that, that wasn't there. I wasn't a player to watch. Mal was an end product as well, but he got it from other places. We used to fight for the six-yard box; we used to fight one another. Many a time I've gone diving in at the near post and it's hit the post and come back out. He's standing there and he knocks it in the back of the net.'

Football has always been noted for its highs and lows. John's experiences were no different.

'Obviously I've got to say Hillsborough, it was phenomenal, although I thought we were crap. In the first 45 minutes we were awful, we were crap, but it was like us. At Forest, again we were crap for 40 minutes. Mal and I couldn't get a kick for the first 25 minutes, basically because they just shut us down. They knew that everything went through Hibbitt, so they just shut us down. So without that service, we were quite happy just to sit back. But how we came out of it at Forest, once we got playing, getting the ball forward a bit better, nobody could live with us. Of course at Hillsborough again, if it had been a boxing match, I think the referee would have stopped it after 40 minutes because we were being battered. But the game is 90 minutes and when you've got somebody like Macdonald around, and somebody like Hibbitt around, who could get the ball out, things can change.

'Bad days, I suppose I would have to say Hereford. I'd love to have had another crack at the FA Cup final. That was the most

disappointing weekend of my life. And not being able to play any more. Disappointing days are when you're told, "We think you might want to move on because you're not going to get a game here." That was when Gordon Lee came. I'd had a word with Joe Harvey about getting into management and things like that, coaching. But they're disappointing days when you realise that you can't do what you want to do any longer, and you can't achieve what you want to any longer.'

During his time with Newcastle United, John scored 73 goals and he chose to highlight two that he felt were a little bit special.

'I've got two actually that stick out as being a little bit more special than any others. I could say the Forest goal, the diving header, but that was easy, I was only six yards out. But there was one against Manchester United. They had just bought Ted MacDougall from Bournemouth, I think for £100,000, and they came to town. They had Best, Charlton, Kidd, MacDougall,

Crerand, Stepney, to name but a few. We won 2–1. I scored with a header from a corner. Hibbitt played a short corner, somebody went out and tapped it back to him. He clipped this thing in and I got up on the penalty spot and powered this header in the net. Timing and everything was **** hot.

'The other one was the same sort of thing which was at Liverpool. I think we drew with Liverpool or beat them at Anfield. Somebody cracked one in from way out wide on the right-hand side, I don't know who it was. They bombed it in and I got up above Hughes and Thompson and whacked a header in at the far post. That again was when I got all the timing right because I worked hard at that, coming in, timing, leaping and getting a jump at the ball. But they stand out. With my feet, forget it, they were tap-ins. I remember a classic, it would be right about the end when I was done. We went to Stoke on a very bad night with the reserves; it was a very bad night. I scored with a bicycle kick from the edge of the box from a cross from somebody. It got a deflection and came behind me. I turned round and did a bicycle on it. I caught it on the end of my toe and it shot in the back of the net from the edge of the box. That would probably go down as something special, but when it's ******* down with rain, blowing a gale, and there's nobody there…'.

Playing as a striker, John came up against some tough defenders over the years. Not surprisingly he started his summary with Leeds United.

'I could compete with Jack Charlton and Norman Hunter, although you always needed to know where Norman was, because if you didn't, he just clattered you. He clattered me once and he nailed me. But I could compete with most people; it didn't really bother me. Charlie Hurley once paid me the ultimate compliment. He said, "Who the hell was that I just played against?" because I gave him the run-around. He was just about done anyway, but I ran the ******** off him. But that was a compliment. I always used to say that Nobby Stiles was difficult to play against, but I never really got amongst him. As a defender, if Best was running at you, you'd **** yourself. But it never really bothered me. I used to have some classic battles against a guy, Hunter from Ipswich. He was an Irish international, used to play at the back, and he was a hard *******. But I gave as good back. I always used to score goals against the Leeds of this world, the big guys. If I could get my timing right, I could get in front of them or I could lead them in and then get behind them. I was always taught to go that way and then check this way, get behind them. I was always watching for gaps that I could get through. It never really bothered me. It bothered me when you get blitzed when you're running in and a goalie whacks you.'

As already highlighted, John took time to settle at Newcastle United and the supporters took time to appreciate what he could achieve.

'During that spell when I first came, I took almighty **** because obviously I was full of beans, watch me score goals. I was top goalscorer at Sheffield United two seasons running, it was just easy. So I thought, this is going to be easy, not knowing what Newcastle was all about. But it didn't work. The pitch was ****, absolute crap, it was just not working. I think I played 10 games before I scored, then I bust my ankle and I was out for a while. I hated it. There was a guy, I bet he's still there actually, on the Popular side before they built the stand, edge of the 18-yard box, flat cap, white scarf, in fact they all had them on. But this guy used to give me no end of ****, absolutely no end of ****. I picked him out all the time. I was out there one night and I made a complete ******** down the line and the **** he gave me. I was there about 10 minutes later and this ball came and it came past me. I'd always marvelled at watching Jimmy Smith play. He did this silly little flick with the outside of his foot and he flicked it that way. It came rolling in to me and I went to feint that way and this guy's cap was there. It was a bigger cap and a bigger scarf, and he was right in front of me. I just flicked this ball and I think Barrowclough got it behind me and crossed it, and they started taking the ****. I stood in front of them, while the game was going on, and I just kept blowing kisses.

'After that it changed, I had a bit of a purple patch. I think at the end of the day, our friend Geordie public appreciate people who work hard and work hard despite what's going on around them. Like I say, I was never a pretty player, a player who's going to pull rabbits out of a hat, like Smithy. Tommy Gibb used to go through the same situation because he wasn't particularly skilful, but he worked his plums off. I was always told if you work hard, you'll go places. I worked hard and kept going, and when things were down, I had to keep shaking myself to get up. I must admit that there were times when I tried to get out of it; I needed help. There were times when I would have cheerfully gone. I went to the boss a couple of times and said, "I need to be away from this lot". But he wouldn't have anything to do with it. He used to say, "No, you're here as long as Macdonald's here, you're here because you make Macdonald work."

'Mal was the turn, when Mal came it all changed. I'd heard of him, I played against him for Sheffield United during the previous season and he frightened me. While we were on the field, he was having a go at Eddie Colquhoun, who was then the Scottish international centre-back, Under-23s, because he was taking jibes out of Mal for his laziness. It was his laziness that got him into these exposed areas because he didn't run about a lot, he stood around. If you're a defender and the centre-forward's standing around, you're either standing or covering. Well, most people cover, so you're a long way away and he'd get away from you. If he got away from you, you were dead. Well, Eddie was taking the **** out of him and some of the other guys were. He erupted twice and scored two goals against us. I don't know what the result was but

Mal scored against us because he was just prolific. It didn't matter where he was; he scored goals. It wasn't the prettiest sight in the world, some of them.'

Once accepted by the Toon Army, John was honoured to have a chant of his own, 'Halleluiah, John Tudor, John Tudor'.

'I don't know where that came from, but it was nice. After that first season, that first 18 months, it was nice. Nowadays you're not given five minutes. You've got to be an instant hit or you're knackered. People keep asking me if I'd like to get back into it. I would, but I don't think I could, I'd be too nice. I couldn't be a *******. I couldn't go out there and do what they do now. I wouldn't last five minutes.'

John went to Wembley with Newcastle United in May 1974 and played in the FA Cup final. Losing 3-0 to Liverpool that day was for John an occasion that he would rather forget.

'We all embarrassed ourselves sometimes when we went out on a Saturday. The FA Cup final was an embarrassment from start to finish. It was an absolutely mismanaged, horrendous two or three weeks. We played Burnley, we get beaten off the field, played to death, and we get to the final. We've got six weeks to get to the Cup final and we've got six or seven games. We played Burnley again the last game but one and we actually got a point. The last game we lost. It was like being on a merry-go-round and I think how that was done was an embarrassment. It was an embarrassment to me as a professional person now, but obviously then it wasn't so bad. But now I realise how bad it was, how badly mismanaged it was. We were at dinners, press occasions, we went to Lords cricket ground and did some stuff there. It was a complete cock-up. Then, the most embarrassing part of it, they kept it a secret that we were going to wear this special tracksuit that was being made by the Burton people. They'd had a competition and some woman had designed this tracksuit that we were supposed to run out at Wembley in. Well, it was one of these ponchos, it was a poncho with no arms. We looked like Batman. So on the Thursday or Friday we refused to wear it. So quickly through one of the guys, I think it was Mal, we got Nike to deliver those bloody purple things, purple and yellow things that were horrendous anyway. It was the only thing we could get at short notice and I think that summed us up for what we were.

'I suppose you've got to point the finger at Joe, you've got to point the finger at the organisation, but we were never treated like proper football players, players with respect, in those days. That's why it all had to change. Hopefully that doesn't happen again now or will not happen again because it is totally out of order. That for me was the embarrassment of actually going home. Emelyn Hughes went on television and said, "That was the easiest day of my life." I was thinking, what does that say to us as a losing finalist? It says a lot and for me that was embarrassing, that was really embarrassing. On the day, it was the day. You can't take anything away from the spectacle and the excitement of being a week down in London, doing all the stuff and going to Wembley. We went on the Thursday actually to have a look around and get the feel of it. Then we went back again on the Saturday, got the feel of it, but looking back that will haunt me. The Hereford game was insignificant, you know, on the day anybody can do anything to anybody. Look what happened the very next Saturday, we went to Manchester United and played them to death. We didn't just beat them; we played them to death. But that was us: one day down, the next day up. I suppose you've got to laugh at what we did that day.'

The late Terry Hibbitt was a talented player and he was also a lively character. John recalled one of many stories involving Hibby.

'A funny time was seeing Terry Hibbitt's face when Malcolm wanted to kill him at Wolverhampton. That was funny when I look at it now but it was serious on the day. But if you could imagine Terry Hibbitt hitting these cracking balls up the front and Malcolm doesn't want to run for them because he doesn't do volleys. Terry could cause a row in an empty house and he wasn't pretty with his language. Seeing his face when Malcolm gets him in the dressing room and I'm hanging onto him, pulling him away, and his strength is coming through. He's picking him up and shoving him against the wall to hang him on a coat hook. That was funny afterwards, scary on the day, but it was funny. Terry was a character, God bless him, a super player, but what a pain in the **** he was, a complete and utter pain. And he didn't mind telling people. He wouldn't keep it to himself, he told everybody. For a little fella he had a big voice, and everybody knew. He wasn't very good at keeping the swear words down.'

When John finished playing football in England in 1994, he moved to Minnesota in the USA. He has lived there ever since and is now the Director of Coaching for Tonka United.

'Tonka United is a community programme, a community-based project, and I've been there for 10 years now. In 1994, I joined them full-time. I've worked with them for 13 years. I went in 1991 originally, just on a pilot thing for a month. In 1992, I went for three months, in 1993 I went for three months, and in 1994 I went permanently, and I've been ever since. It's like Wallsend Boys Club but we have girls. I've got 56 teams playing at various age groups and they travel out into the community.'

By his own admission John's style of play was not pretty to watch. He considered himself to be an end product on the football field. Those who saw John play regularly would perhaps say that he eventually became the finished article during his spell at St James' Park. Playing alongside Malcolm Macdonald, John was encouraged to get his teeth into games. Fortunately for John, he didn't have to leave his in a glass in the dressing room.

Chapter 8
MICKY BURNS
(1974–78)

MICHAEL EDWARD BURNS was born on 21 December 1946 in Preston, Lancashire. A striker signed from Blackpool in June 1974 for £170,000, Micky made 189 senior starts for Newcastle United and scored 51 goals. His interest in sport began like so many at school.

'Well, I actually played most sports at school. It really started at school: junior school and then at secondary school. At secondary school the two main sports were football and cricket. So it was football in the winter and cricket, with a little bit of athletics and cross-country, in the summer. I represented the school in a number of sports, but football was always my number one sport. So I grew up really playing football in the winter and cricket in the summer. It all just developed through school and through the schoolboys system. Since I'm from Preston, my hero as a kid was obviously Tom Finney. I watched Preston from being a very young boy and he was the hero in that era. He was the only one for me when I was growing up.'

Micky's football career started very early but it had to compete with his education, as he explained.

'I played for St Joseph's in the Preston and District Catholic League, both at under-18s and at senior level as well. That was until sort of 16, 17 years. Then I went to play amateur for a team that was then in the Lancashire Combination League, a team called Chorley, in what was really a semi-professional league, but I played as an amateur. I played for them for about 18 months and was chosen to play for Lancashire amateurs. I was still at school doing my A levels. It was indicated to me that if I wanted to go on to play at international level as an amateur that I would need to move to an amateur club. Chorley at that time was semi-professional. So I moved on to Skelmersdale and I had five good years there while I was in the sixth form and at university.

'I came out of university at 21. I taught in Liverpool for a year at a secondary school, Warbreck Secondary. I did a year, which I had to do then if I wanted to teach, because you had to do a probationary year. To get your teaching certificate in those days, you did a three years university course then a year's probation. There had been a number of professional football clubs interested in me, but while I was at university I wasn't interested in them. At the end of my probation year there was still some interest. I was playing amateur football for Skelmersdale and I got into the England side as an amateur. But after a year of teaching and playing for England as an amateur, a number of professional clubs

offered me the opportunity to turn professional. I suppose at the time I wanted to know if I could really play at that level. I decided that I was going to give it a go for a year, take a year out of teaching, and see if I could make it in the professional ranks. I went to Blackpool and subsequently spent five years there, one year in the old First Division and four in the old Second Division. Then Newcastle came in for me.'

Micky moved to Newcastle United in June 1974 and followed in the footsteps of a fellow Blackpool colleague.

'Blackpool at that time was a team that more or less sold a player a year and I suppose that it was my turn. I mean, Tony Green and Tommy Hutchinson had gone in the previous two years; Tony obviously to Newcastle and Tommy went to Coventry. We had just missed out on promotion to the First Division. I think that we had finished third. We lost our last match at Sunderland. Had we won it, we would have had a chance of going up. But we lost the game 2–1. Then I got a phone call from Harry Potts, who was the manager of Blackpool, asking me to meet him on the M6, telling me that somebody wanted to talk to me. It just happened to be Joe Harvey. It was at Charnock Richard service station on the M6. It was more or less done and dusted in a couple of hours in an afternoon.

'I travelled up the following day for a medical. We agreed terms, the two clubs agreed terms and I signed the contract. For the medical, Alec Mutch took me down to see the doctor. I had a few X-rays and that was all done in a couple of hours.

'It was the middle of the summer break when I signed, so obviously I went home then until the pre-season training. I put my house up for sale and started to look for a house in Newcastle. I hadn't found one quick enough for the start of July when I reported back to the club because I had to sell the one back in Blackpool. I eventually sold the one in Blackpool and found a house in Newcastle, but I stayed in the County Hotel for about three months, which was a bit of an ordeal because I had two young children. My youngest was only months old and my daughter was two and a half. So it was a bit difficult, with me being in a hotel all week in Newcastle and the family being back in Blackpool. But eventually we found a house and moved in. I lived at Throckley Bank Top.'

Having swapped the North West for the North East, I asked

Micky about his memories of St James' Park, the training and match days.

'My memory of the stadium was how open it was and what a tremendous atmosphere it had. With it being so open, it had an atmosphere that you didn't normally get with the more enclosed stadiums. But it got a bit hairy when the weather wasn't too good and the wind blew. That was one of my most vivid memories of moving to the North East: the first winter and the old east wind blowing. It was a bit chilly, I can tell you. We had training at Benwell and it was a bit sparse, to say the least. Originally, there were just the changing rooms when you got there, then open expanse with a couple of pitches on it. Then they built an indoor sort of area where it was a little bit better for the winter months. I think that was really needed at the time with the winters that they used to get at Newcastle. They don't seem to get the same winters nowadays. On match days I always had fish and mashed potatoes for lunch. That was my pre-match meal at home for home games. Obviously for away games we would be in a hotel. There were no superstitions.'

Micky's home debut for Newcastle United was actually playing in a Texaco Cup game against Teesside rivals Middlesbrough. He scored a marvellous goal, making a solo run from halfway and beating several opponents before finding the net. It was the first of many memorable games and goals.

'That's right, my first game was against Middlesbrough. It was a sort of dream debut, if you will. I mean, it just happens, you have your good days and your bad days, and it just happened that I had a good day on my debut. It was quite a full stadium with it being a local derby. It was one of those goals, you go and beat a few players and I just rolled it in. I think the League Cup final in 1976 was special, even though we lost. It was my first trip as a professional to Wembley. I'd played there before as an amateur. I think it's always memorable when you get to the cup finals. The result was a bit disappointing on the day. I think that was probably the most memorable game.

'All home games were special. The Newcastle fans have always been renowned for their passion and their noise, and they were very close to you. With it being an open stadium, it made it look closer and it was predominantly standing then. There were only just the two stands. When the modern stands are full I don't think the stadiums look as imposing as they used to do. It's maybe because they're not packed in so tightly.

'I can remember the first game of the season when Richard Dinnis was in charge and we beat Leeds 3–2. I got a couple of goals that day, but then we went down that season strangely enough. Leeds were a good side at the time. It was the first game of the season, you know, I got a couple of goals, it was Richard's first game in charge, and then it all went downhill from there. I mean, that game stands out, but there were a few games during the year before when we got into Europe with Gordon Lee in charge. There were a few games that year that were memorable. We got some good results, beating Liverpool at home 1–0. Liverpool were really the top side in the country at the time. I think Paul Cannell scored actually.

'I spent most of my time at Newcastle as a sort of third striker, playing from central midfield, just behind the two strikers. It was similar to the diamond pattern played by a number of clubs nowadays, where they played two strikers, with no winger, with the third striker on the top of the diamond. That system worked quite well for us. I think it was Alan Gowling and Malcolm Macdonald up front and then when Malcolm left, Paul Cannell came in.'

Micky had fond memories of the Toon Army and was honoured to have his own chant which on its earthiest rendition was, 'He's here, he's there, he's every ******* where, Micky Burns'.

'They were tremendous supporters, very friendly. During the years that I spent in the North East, the friendliness of the people really stood out. In those days I don't think it was as intense as it is now. Most Saturday nights after the game, I would go out with my wife and a couple of friends into the Bigg Market and have a curry, and nobody bothered me at all. I don't think that is quite as open to players now. Yes, I remember the chant. Somebody made a record of it. I wasn't aware of it, but I was invited up as guest and I came to a game: it was probably about seven or eight years ago or more. I came up for the game and they were playing it.'

During his playing career at St James' Park, Micky experienced a number of different managers with different styles. He was one of the players at the centre of what was known at the time as the 'Players' Revolt'. Micky explained the developments leading up to the event and charts the managerial history of the club during his time with Newcastle United.

'I think that Newcastle had started to take off a little bit. Under Joe Harvey we were a very cavalier side. We would win the majority of our home games in cavalier style, but away from home we struggled. I think it was because of the style of our play. I didn't think that we were ever going to win anything or get near to winning anything, simply because we weren't strong enough away from home defensively. It was a very cavalier approach to the game, but I suppose that was traditional with Newcastle at the time; I can appreciate that.

'I think when Gordon [Lee] came, he recognised that and he looked for a more hard-working, more organised team, with a less cavalier and a more professional approach. People will remember the famous "stars are in the sky" comment. It was unfortunate, I'd been very friendly with Malcolm [Macdonald] for many years at Newcastle and afterwards as well, but he didn't fit into that mould. I think that was why Gordon eventually sold him because he couldn't fit into the mould and the type of game that he wanted to play. The unfortunate part with Gordon was that he didn't buy any replacements. If you look at that squad that got into Europe, they did it with 13 or 14 players. You were competing against teams who had squads of 16, 17 and 18 at that time, which seems small when compared to today. We were lucky in many respects with the injuries that year; we didn't get a lot of injuries and we did very well. But I think Gordon didn't move on. Well, he did move on, he went off to Everton. Then Richard [Dinnis] took over and we went down the following season.

'The so-called "Players' Revolt" – a lot of that got misreported as well at the time. We talk about player power and all sorts; there was no real player power. A lot of it came out of the fact that a lot of players were out of contract the same year. What the board at the time tried to do was to pick them off one at a time, but the players got together and said, "No, we're not having that". There were one or two quite intelligent lads on the books and they helped to move the players as well. But it wasn't really player power. The main thing was about contracts. It wasn't about managers or anything like that; it was about contracts. When he got the job, Richard had to sort out the contracts. At the end of the day they called it the Players' Revolt that appointed Richard, but the board made the decision to appoint Richard Dinnis. The players didn't make that appointment.

'The only thing that happened, when Gordon Lee left, was that they asked four senior players, of which I was one, to go and speak to two of the directors to talk about what they felt should happen. All we asked for was that there was some continuity. We were going well at the time, I think. You would need to speak to Gordon on why he left, but I suspect that it would be something to do with the fact that he wasn't getting the support within the club. I think that he felt without support that he wasn't going to stay. It was unfortunate that he left at that time because I think, had he strengthened that squad, there was every possibility we could have gone on to do better things. But history will tell you that it didn't happen.

Chapter 8: MICKY BURNS

'They brought in a supposedly hard manager after Richard, Bill McGarry. It was no secret that we didn't get on. To be fair, my contract was up at the end of that year and he called me and asked me to sign another contract. He had got rid of all the other senior players – Alan Gowling, Geoff Nulty, Tommy Craig – and I was sort of the one left. He wanted me to stay but too much water had gone under the bridge by then and I said that I didn't feel that I wanted to sign another contract. I wanted to move on. But he did try to persuade me, so it wasn't as though he got rid of me. I got the opportunity to go to Cardiff as player-coach, which unfortunately didn't work out for me. I finished up three or four months later back at Middlesbrough and I had three years there before I retired. Middlesbrough were a good side at that time, they had some good young players.'

During his career with Newcastle United, Micky scored 51 goals. Some of these were quite spectacular, but one in particular he has tried hard to forget.

'My most embarrassing moment was when we came back from the League Cup final. We played Stoke City on the Wednesday in a League game and we lost 1–0 and I scored an own goal. It was the only own goal that I ever scored in my career. It was a bit embarrassing really because it was a full house at St James' Park after the League Cup final. We had a bad day on that Wednesday. We had a really bad day against Stoke. The ball came off my knee from a corner. Somebody headed it and it came off my knee. It was embarrassing.'

Fortunately for Micky he will always be remembered for the goals that he scored at the other end of the pitch. He looked back on his time at Newcastle United with great fondness.

'I don't think that I would have changed them for the world. I was 27 to 31, which is really the best part of your career. I was at my fittest and the maturist as a player. I had sort of six, seven years as a professional and I felt that those were the best years of my football career. Whilst I was there, the crowd and the public were excellent with me and I wouldn't hear any criticism of them. The Newcastle United fan base is fantastic, absolutely fantastic, the reception that they give the players. Thinking about my football career, the way that the Newcastle fans treat the players as well, on and off the pitch, will live with me for the rest of my life.'

Following the departure of Malcolm Macdonald from Newcastle United to Arsenal in August 1976, Micky was the club's top goalscorer during the next two consecutive seasons. He scored some great goals and it really was a case of him being 'here, there, and every ******* where'.

Chapter 9

MICK MARTIN
(1978–83)

MICHAEL PAUL MARTIN was born in Dublin on 9 July 1951. Signed from West Bromwich Albion in November 1978 for £100,000, Mick was a midfield player who made 155 senior starts for Newcastle United and scored six goals. He gained 52 full international caps playing for the Republic of Ireland. Playing football was very much in Mick's blood.

'Well, I probably had a more interesting start than most people. My father was an ex-professional footballer; he played for Aston Villa. He signed for Leeds first in 1946 and then the following year he moved from Leeds to Aston Villa. He spent the rest of his career at Aston Villa, which spanned nine years. Then he went back to Ireland in 1957, having played for 11 years in England as a full-time professional. So I would assume that I inherited some form of gene that he had and eventually got into the business, or more into the profession – although he was a different build to me. He was a big strapping centre-half, about six foot three, six foot four. He doubled up as a goalkeeper, funnily enough. He was so good that he also played in goal.

'I was always struggling as a young fella because in my age group, 13s and 14s, they were always two or three inches bigger than me. I was quite small. I suddenly got bigger when I was 16, 17. I was never involved at international level as a schoolboy because I was too small. But when I got older, it all started to come through then. So from that point of view it would have been inherited. Well, I assume that it was inherited.'

Although Mick's professional career was established in England, the roots of his football were to be found back in Ireland.

'My early career, it all stemmed back in Dublin when I played for probably the best junior side in Ireland, Home Farm, who produced a lot of the great players who came to England over the years, going back before me. Then after me, there are the likes of Ian Harte, young Kelly at Leeds and Richard Dunne now at Manchester City. All those players genuinely got treated well by a top club like that. I was no different. I went from Home Farm to Bohemians, who were in the League of Ireland, which was the top League in Ireland, as a 17, 18 year old. I progressed there from their Under-18s to the reserves and into the first team, where I got established for two or three years.

'Then I caught the eye of people in England and I came across to England. Manchester United signed me in January 1973. Tommy Docherty was the manager, Pat Crerand was the assistant manager and Matt Busby was a director at the club, but he was not officially involved. I came across with my father, having played on a Sunday in Dublin for Bohemians against Shelbourne: we beat them 3–0. Tommy Docherty was there with Pat Crerand looking at another player. After the game he came across to one of the scouts and said, "How come he's been here and no one's sent him over to me?" So, at that time I was playing well and I had a lot of interest from England. Clubs were ringing up and asking me to come over for trials, but at that time I had already been an international as well, so people would or should have known what I could do. I wasn't prepared to come over and let them have a look at me because they would have known about me.

'So Manchester United decided that they wanted me and I came over. They saw me on the Sunday, I came over on the Tuesday, signed for them on the Tuesday, and I left my job as a sports shop manager in Dublin. That was all of 32 years ago and I've been here in England ever since. I had two and a half years at Manchester United, but it was not through the most successful period of their history. They got relegated under Tommy Docherty, and then promoted under Tommy Docherty the same season I was involved, although not in a lot of games. I played 40 times for Manchester United over the two and a half years. I kind of fell out with the manager for him not playing me more than he should have done.

'So in the end I moved down to West Bromwich Albion in October 1975 and signed for them. Johnny Giles was the manager, which made it easier for me to join because he was a Dublin boy. He was the manager of the national side and a team colleague of mine. He wanted me there because he wanted to play me. They were in the old Second Division at the time. Johnny had left Leeds United, he had got the job at West Brom and he obviously looked for people who he thought could be successful. I went to West

Brom in the October and they were third from the bottom of the League. They got promoted by the end of the season. We had a great run from third from the bottom and we got promoted on the last day of the season to the old First Division in 1976.

'I came up to Newcastle after a period at West Brom when I had the best part of my career. We had been successful; we had been promoted. We finished in the top six most of the time during the period that I was there. We had three managers, mind. Johnny Giles left and went to Vancouver Whitecaps. Ronnie Allen, the ex-West Brom player, came in as a manager and did quite well. Then he went to Saudi Arabia, having been offered a good job. Then Ron Atkinson came in and did a very good job.'

Mick was transferred to Newcastle United in 1978 after some reluctance on the part of West Bromwich Albion to sell him.

'West Brom didn't want me to go. It was a case of Newcastle wanted me. I remember it very well. Ron Atkinson had informed me, along with the chairman, and they told me that Newcastle and Wolverhampton Wanderers wanted me. They knew that I was sellable because they had good players there and there were younger players putting pressure on. So there was a surplus of players. They never said that I was available, but when an offer came in, they were bound to let me know. So they rang me up one day and Ron Atkinson said, "Come in and speak to me. Newcastle have been on the phone. They want to sign you, but we're not over keen for you to go. But the choice is yours because they've offered reasonable terms and reasonable money." So I went to the club at two o'clock and spoke to Ron Atkinson. I obviously wanted the deal to be right for me. I wanted "x" amount of money to go. The "x" amount of money wasn't forthcoming so Ron says, "Look, Newcastle won't pay that excess and we're not prepared to pay it because we don't want you to go. We're quite happy for you to stay." I said, "Fine, Ron, no problem. I'm off home now, that's it."

Chapter 9: MICK MARTIN

'When I got home, the phone had rung for me. It was Ron saying that Newcastle had decided that they would pay the sort of money I was asking for. So I had to get back in the car and drive back to the club. This time I was told, "You'd better bring some clothes with you because you might have to go straight up there." So I went back to West Brom and spoke to Newcastle. They had asked if I would go up on that night, go up and speak to them the following day. So I took some clothes, went to the club and spoke to Ron. He said, "The chairman says you're good here, you're good for the team, morale is good, you're a good personality, but do whatever you want to do." I came up to Newcastle, spoke to them, spoke to some friends, and decided after 24 hours that Newcastle United would be a good move career-wise. And that's how it happened.'

Mick can be found at St James' Park for all Newcastle United home games and can be heard on local radio co-commentating. The stadium has changed vastly since his playing days, so I asked him to cast his mind back to the late 1970s.

'It was fairly straightforward. You had the two ends, the Gallowgate and the Leazes End. You had the old stand nearside, but the other stand was as it is now. The East Stand is virtually as it was. But obviously the changing rooms, the corporate facilities, the directors' room and all that have changed. The whole surrounding has changed as it would do to facilitate this new stadium of 52,000. It was always a good place to come and play. The atmosphere was good, the people were good, but like everything else, that's changed. The stadium was old and as time had gone by they had to take bits and pieces down. The old West Stand, now the Milburn Stand, wouldn't have taken a lot of knocking down, because it was the old wooden structure. It needed doing and look at what happened afterwards; they went above that level.

'It was necessary to do stuff like that. It was a stadium that was old. I would have seen the old footage of *Match of the Day* on a

Saturday night, even before I came to England, and you would see St James' Park. You had a clock at the top part. You knew where you were at; you were at St James' Park. It was good, I enjoyed being part of a club that harboured the names of great people of the past. It was the same at Old Trafford. I always thought that I was very fortunate to play for a club like that, to get changed beside the likes of Bobby Charlton, Denis Law, which I did when I came to England. Then to go to St James' Park, thinking "Jackie Milburn would have changed in here, and Malcolm Macdonald, people like that". So from that point of view I felt privileged.'

Newcastle United have a purpose-built training facility nowadays which is vastly different to when Mick played. However, he believes that the basics may not have changed all that much in spite of the improved surroundings.

'Training I don't think has changed an awful lot. It would have changed a lot between my father's period and my period. He played in the mid-50s and my career span was sort of the mid-70s through to the mid-80s. When he was training, the old trainer used to come out in a pair of runners and say, "Right lads, run around that training field for 12 laps." When you'd finished that, he'd be sitting there having a smoke. But training in the mid-70s was kind of well in advance, I felt, and was getting more advanced as weeks went by. The facilities weren't great I have to say. At West Brom we got changed and we had a facility across the road which was owned by the club. It had a nice bit of grass, a pitch, and a couple of five-a-sides. That was it, no gym or anything like that. The physio's room was two tables which were in the dressing room. Manchester United were quite in advance of a lot of clubs because they were still classified as probably the biggest club around, name-wise, and the facilities were very good, far better than West Brom. It didn't mean that they were a better team, but the training facilities were far better.

'Coming up to Newcastle, the training at Benwell, compared to now, the facilities were nothing compared to what the players have now. Compared to other teams then, the facilities weren't bad. Going back 20 years before I came, the old director Fenton Braithwaite had bought it from maybe the Coal Board and it was used solely for training our teams. It was good enough. It was heavy when the weather got bad, but they had an indoor facility, and they had weights and a multigym, otherwise you were outside. But the training facilities weren't as good as they should have been. It didn't bother us all that much.

'Everybody remembers Ronnie, old Ronnie – I got on very well with him. He also worked on the match days down at St James' Park. You'd go in and Ronnie would be there. I always used to bring him back a bottle of whisky when I was away on international games. He always liked that. He would never mention it to me, but I would always bring one back because he looked after us. He worked up until not so long ago. But he was nice, a good lad, he looked after us well. He would make a big pot of tea and that was your total luxury that you had coming to training. Now you get your breakfast, lunch and evening meal at the facility that they have. Sometimes at other grounds you'd ask for a pot of tea and they would sort of growl at you, "You want a cup of tea?" The atmosphere was good at training and the facilities were okay. But compared to what they have now, they are miles and miles away from what it was like. I'm not saying that the training techniques are any different now, to be honest with you.'

Reading accounts of Mick's career with Newcastle United in other publications, it is generally suggested that he had a slow start. I asked Mick for his thoughts about this.

'My home debut, I think my first game at home…my first game was Crystal Palace away. I can't remember my first game at home. It might have been QPR. I wouldn't necessarily think that I had a slow start. I was bought by the club, by Bill McGarry and the chairman Stan Seymour, with the specific view to be captain and on the back of being captain, we needed to get promotion

back to the old First Division. Now it came too late because by the time I'd come up, it was almost Christmas. Terry Hibbitt was still playing and he was captain. McGarry was trying to get players in to get the job done. By the end of the season we were ordinary, not only me but a lot of the other players. It was very hard coming from the old First Division, having played three or four years on the trot and having been successful without winning anything, but you were always in the top six. I was going down to probably a bigger club who were struggling like hell to get back there. But I wouldn't necessarily say I was struggling performance-wise.

'To be fair, I think that it is very difficult to come to a club and be a hit straight away. You've got to settle into the area, just like you do now, and it's very difficult. Anyway, at the end of that season we finished something like seventh. We started the following season on the pre-season and McGarry took me to one side and says, "I'm going to make you the new captain of the club because we need to push on from here. We need to go and get promotion. We look as if we've got a chance. We've got some players at that level." We didn't have a bad squad at the time. Peter Withe was a very good player. Alan Shoulder was starting to impress. You had John Connolly and the likes of John Brownlie, Hibby was still there, Tommy Cassidy was still around and there was myself. So it was quite good in terms of that level of football. A lot of these players had played at the top level also, having shone at a big club and trying to get themselves back.

'We were going along great until the Christmas that year and we were three points clear at the top of the League. I thought that I was quite influential in the way things were going. But I got a bad injury at Luton in the December 1980 that knocked me out for 11 months and we just basically seemed to plummet after that. We played Luton on the day that I got injured. I got a very serious medial ligament injury which kept me out for 11 months. From that period of being three points clear at the top of the League, we finished up to be a very ordinary seventh. Sunderland at that time I think were nine points adrift of us and they finished getting promotion. We finished well down, having beaten them on New Year's Day. I was in hospital at the time when we beat them 3–1. And I thought, well that's us, now we're back, you know. But the second half of the season was horrendous; we just lost all sorts of leadership.

'A lot of people and the manager said to me, "If you'd been fit for the rest of that season, Newcastle would have been back in the First Division far quicker than they were." It took them until Kevin Keegan came along to get back in. I think we would have got promoted if I'd stayed fit. That was basically it. I got back fit, I got the captaincy, got back involved in the club, got back into international football, and I was quite enjoying it and playing well. The club was always hovering on the fourth or fifth position and couldn't quite get there. In many ways it was disappointing for us as a club, but then Kevin Keegan came along. It was quite a big signing for the club and no one believed it. I was in Madeira on the pre-season training with Newcastle when it happened. One of the directors, Ronnie McKenzie, came up to me and said, "I'll need to speak to you. Keep it quiet, we're signing Kevin Keegan tomorrow morning." I just said, "Oh, bloody hell, I didn't catch wind of that, no one told me. Normally I hear things. Keegan to come here would be great for the club."

'The following day it was announced that Keegan had signed. I knew the club was such a club that needed a character or a person of that nature to get it going again. Kevin came and full credit to Arthur Cox for getting him. It did bring a lot of atmosphere into the club, but it didn't make any difference to the way the club responded. In that first year he had difficulty settling into the type of football it was. I remember playing with Kevin that year. He said, "If you play like that every week, I'm going to struggle like hell. I'll never get to kick the ball. It's all up in the air." I said, "I felt the same in the first year too. You've just got to adapt and accept that you're not playing at Liverpool or Hamburg any more. It's Newcastle United and it's in the Second Division." He probably came to realise that in the second year. At the end of that first year when Kevin came, I'd gone.'

Mick was given the nickname 'Zico' when playing for Newcastle United and I asked him if he knew of its origins.

'No idea. Around the time, halfway through that first season, I think Arthur Cox had played Nigel Walker instead of me. It might have been someone else, but I wasn't playing, I was on the bench. When I came on, I was doing particularly well. Zico was a forward for a start and I was a central midfielder. One or two people said it must have started then, but I said if it was then, why did it start and where did the Zico thing come from? It just came. While I thoroughly enjoyed it and I used to enjoy the banter with the crowd – I got on very well with the crowd at that stage – there was a period prior to it when there was a section of the crowd that were a bit heavy with me sometimes. I didn't mind that because they're entitled to do that. I got one or two strange letters in the post as well – as players do from time to time. But I forgot all about that and I got on with it. The Zico thing has stuck to me until now. Wherever I go, people tend to recognise me, not only my face but also my voice because I do the radio stuff, and they're still keen to speak to me. They're very keen to talk about the current team just as much as to talk about my times at the club. It's good.'

During his days at St James' Park, Mick managed to score six goals and I wondered if he could recall them all.

'Funnily enough, one was on the television at the weekend. Tyne Tees were on to me saying, "Did you watch our little bit of nostalgia last night?" I said, "No I didn't". They said, "Oh, we had a game that you played in against Charlton Athletic, which was 25 years ago last Saturday's game." I remember the game well. We beat them 5–3 and I scored and made a couple in the game. I wouldn't mind having a look at the tape because I wasn't a prolific goalscorer. My job at Newcastle was becoming very much a holding player and an organiser, whereas at Manchester United and West Bromwich Albion I had a kind of freedom, more so at West Brom. I think I scored nine goals in one season as a central midfield player, with the specific job to get forward into the box and score goals.

'But then as I got older and I came to Newcastle, my job was such as, "Right, you're in charge". I liked being in charge; I liked telling people what to do on the field. I liked to be around the hub of the ball and I liked that responsibility, like Rob Lee had. You dictate where the game is going, if things are good. I remember scoring a goal against Sheffield Wednesday up here which was a header. I think it might have been a cup game. It was a good goal; I enjoyed it. I remember scoring against Bolton up here, Blackburn away, but they were few and far between. Six goals in 150-odd games is not an awful lot. But when you're a holding player, it's not bad. But you wouldn't see the likes of Amdy Faye scoring a lot of goals between now and the end of the year. Rob Lee, when he became that holding player, I bet he only scored two goals in two years, or three goals in two years, whereas before that he used to get forward and score goals.

'That sums it up, 155 games and six goals in a period when Newcastle weren't great, really. We were struggling like hell to get better through the period when Arthur Cox came along after Bill McGarry. We were a very ordinary side, really ordinary. We had the same personnel. A couple of new players had come along. Peter Cartwright had come through, Bobby Shinton had been signed and Ray Clarke had been signed before that. We had smashing fellas but they weren't the greatest players in the world, and they would admit that themselves. I have to say that the standard of player you're playing with makes you a better player. But if they happen to be average players, then it's a lot harder. You would play it into space for forwards to chase and continue the move. But at Newcastle, sometimes when I played it into space, no-one chased the ball. Sometimes they looked at you wondering, 'What's he played it in there for?', and it made a good pass look like a bad pass. And sometimes the crowd would react to it.'

The game of football has changed a lot since Mick played and I asked him if these changes were for the better.

'It's debatable in many ways. I would say it's a lot quicker and it probably looks a lot quicker to the eye. I think the ball travels quicker and that might make it look a bit quicker. And I think the very top sides can play the game at that pace. The ones below them, I don't think are as good. I think the players look after themselves a little bit better than we did. I don't think they're necessarily fitter but I think they look after themselves better. They watch their lives. You see, there's a lot of money in the game now, which means even an extra year or two in the game could mean a difference between a half of a million and a million pounds to a player. You wouldn't have got that in the 12 years that I played football, never mind two years more. So, from that point of view, it's obviously beneficial to look after yourself. Other than that, there are certain rules that have come into the game, such as the backpass where you can't give the ball to the goalkeeper to pick it up. Equipment, I think that the footwear has changed dramatically. Your kit has changed; it's more lightweight. To be honest with you, I never felt I had a heavy shirt on when I went out on a Saturday. All of those things have changed to make the game probably better. I would think the game I played in was just as exciting. There were as many goalmouth thrills as there are now. The best players scored goals that were as good as they score now and they could certainly play now. I would love to be playing now, if I was 30 years younger.'

As a radio co-commentator, Mick is tuned in to the modern-day supporters of Newcastle United and is very much aware of the booing and the abuse vented towards certain players.

'I think the supporter now relates to what players are doing in relation to performances on a Saturday. They'll say, "Well, he's getting paid 10,000, or 20,000, or 40,000 a week and he's crap." I think it's a harsh thing to do to players because I don't think any player goes out not purposely wanting to play well. It's a showbiz game. You go out in front of 52,000 supporters and you think, "I'm going to show these people how I'm going to play." Some days things go your way and it becomes an easy game for you. Other days it's hard and you're running into brick walls, losing the ball and people are slagging you off. It doesn't stop you doing the same things, approaching the game in the same way. It might just be a bad day at the office. You see, when I'm sitting in here running a business on my own, no one sees what I do. No one sees what I do right or wrong. So when I do something wrong, no one sees me. If you make a mistake on a football pitch, 52,000 people are there. On top of that, one million people are watching on a Saturday night and they see you.

'That's why players are paid as well as they are because of the pressure level. And on top of that since football was invented, up to the time of television putting money into the game, the players were abused severely in relation to wages. I think that they may have too much control now. When Newcastle were playing in front of 60,000 people, the club was paying their players £12 a week. They didn't pay them enough and they had to suffer with the injuries, taking them into life after football. Some players became housebound and bedridden because of injured ankles, knees and joints. I don't begrudge the players all the money that they get now. Some of them aren't worth it, but I don't begrudge them.'

All players accumulate stories from their playing days and Mick selected three from three different clubs.

'I'm sure there are loads, really, that happened at a variety of places. I remember touring China. We were the first side to tour China, behind the Iron Curtain, with West Bromwich Albion and it was televised for an hour-long documentary. It was run by BBC2. We went out to China for three weeks and went to Shanghai, Peking and one or two other provincial places. They took a BBC film crew to cover it because we were the first to do it. And I remember doing a little piece – it wasn't embarrassing, it was just a bit of fun. The cameras were there and it was two weeks into the three. You know when you're young enough not to be interested in the Great Wall and all the great things that China had to offer, and all you wanted to do was have a game of cards. I wasn't interested in visiting all the churches that they had. I was sitting there reading out a little story, a letter that I had written to my wife, and it sounded more like a suicide note. It said, "The way things are going, it's more likely that I will commit suicide than ever see you again."

'I remember at Manchester United, the very last game when we got relegated from the First to the Second Division. It was at Old Trafford against Manchester City and Denis Law backheeled the winner. It was the last game of the season and I was sub at the time. I had a Manchester United top, tracksuit bottoms and a baseball cap on. Of course, after the game the entire crowd had come onto the pitch. The riot police came on. I'd just come out of the dugout and I was walking onto the pitch. The police had rushed on and they started hitting me with batons. They thought that I was one of the supporters. They hit me on the back of my leg and on my arm. I had to take my cap off so that the Chief Superintendent could realise that I was one of the players. I thought to myself, "Bloody hell, that was sore".

'At Newcastle I had some great times, bundles of fun. I remember when we were playing Wrexham one night, the match was abandoned because it was so cold, so wet and so miserable at half-time. I think it was a 1–1 draw. Tommy Cassidy scored for us. It was so cold that nobody went to congratulate him. We sort of walked back to the halfway line. We were actually physically numb with the cold. They scored and equalised. Poor Terry Hibbitt, Lord rest his soul, he was like a block of ice and he was a smoker as well. So he went over and got his cigarettes out and you could see him up against the wall, dragging on his cigarette. He says, "I'm not going on". As it happened, the referee came in and said that the game had to be abandoned. There were only 6,000 there that night. You know, it was not your typical Newcastle United. Even if it was a Wednesday night, in those days when we were there, you'd get 18–20,000, a good crowd.'

Mick left Newcastle United in 1983, moving briefly to Wolverhampton Wanderers before joining Vancouver Whitecaps in Canada. He was to return to St James' Park in

1987, becoming chief scout and later assistant coach. He is now settled in the area and runs his own promotions business as well as doing the radio work. Mick can be seen at all Newcastle United home games and is well respected within the club. To many supporters Mick will always be 'Zico' and, as far as Mick was concerned, his best memory of China was the tea made by old Ronnie.

Chapter 10

JOHN ANDERSON
(1982–92)

JOHN CHRISTOPHER PATRICK ANDERSON was born on 7 November 1959 in Dublin, Ireland. A defender signed from Preston North End in August 1982 on a free transfer, John went on to make 322 senior starts for Newcastle United and he scored 15 goals. He gained 16 full international caps playing for his country and one Under-21 cap. John was awarded a testimonial for his services to Newcastle United. The seeds of his football career were very much sown during his childhood, playing in the streets in his native Dublin.

'Basically what happened was, when I was growing up in the early 1960s, whereas nowadays they've all got computers, everybody played football. My dad and my uncles played Gaelic football and I just got into it that way. From as far back as I can remember I was always kicking a ball, even if it was only against a wall. I think that I got a ball every Christmas and one thing and another, and I got encouraged along that way. Back then, after work, the men used to come out and kick the ball and you always just fell in with that. That's basically how it all started. From then I graduated to playing for local teams and that was how it all really started for me.

'I played a lot of Gaelic football when I went to school because back then you couldn't play soccer in Ireland. You either played Gaelic football or hurling. The only way that you could play soccer was to join a local junior side. So the majority of my early years were spent playing Gaelic football and, believe it or not, I always enjoyed playing Gaelic more than I did soccer. Gaelic was always my first love and so I used to play it for the school. I used to play soccer on a Saturday morning for a junior side and then play Gaelic in the afternoon for a junior side. Then I would do the same again on the Sunday. It amazes me nowadays when you hear kids saying that they're tired out playing twice a week, when I used to play four times over the weekend. After school you just used to drop the bag by the back door and you were away playing, kicking a ball around until your mother came shouting because your dinner was on the table.'

When John was growing up in Ireland he had quite a few childhood football heroes.

'Football heroes for me…to start there was probably Johnny Giles. Back then we didn't have televisions, you know. The only people that you really saw were like the internationals when they came. Obviously the well-known ones like Pele and Beckenbauer to a degree. So your heroes were mainly people that you knew, as I've already mentioned, Johnny Giles, Alan Kelly, people like that. Basically the only way that they were your heroes was because you used to bunk off school to go and watch the internationals. Back then they were played in the afternoons because stadiums in Ireland didn't have floodlights. So you used to bunk off school to go and watch the matches and get yourself into all sorts of trouble.

'Other heroes…there was obviously George Best and your Manchester United players. The game didn't have the exposure that it's got now. Because of the Munich Air Disaster everybody had an affection for Manchester United at that time. Nobby Stiles when England won the World Cup, everybody remembered him because of his jig. There was also Bobby Charlton and Denis Law at Manchester United. Then there was the Arsenal side, the double side of the 1970s, with Frank McLintock, Bob McNab, Bob Wilson, those sort of players. Heroes then, you would put them on a different level. I think people nowadays and kids nowadays don't put the modern players on the same level as we put our heroes. I don't think that they have the same respect for the guys today. When you talk about hero worship, I don't think that they respect them as much as we respected ours.

'I remember when Johnny Giles was manager of West Brom, where I first went, and he called at the house. I'd been out and there was this huge car outside. All the kids went, "Johnny Giles is in your house". I walked in and there was this fella sat there. He went, "Hello John, pleased to meet you", and I couldn't speak. I just stood there gobsmacked. Johnny Giles was sitting in my house. You wouldn't speak to him unless he spoke to you and it was "Mr Giles" you know, it wasn't "Johnny". Anybody who was older than you was always "Mr" back then.'

Before moving to and settling in the North East, John's football career took him to the Midlands and Lancashire. However, it all began in Ireland where he attracted the interest of a number of clubs.

'Back then there were scouts everywhere. I went to Coventry, Wolves, West Ham, and I later went to Manchester United every summer holiday for a week. Ronnie Whelan, who later went on to play for Liverpool, and another lad called Derek Carroll; there were three of us used to go every holiday. I finished school at 15 and that summer, because I wasn't going back to school, they asked me to stay for six weeks. At the time I agreed. I came from a little place just outside Dublin – it only had 21 houses – and one thing and another. So being in Manchester it was great because you had the two other boys with you. You always knew that you were going back, so it was something different. But the two other lads left and I was there on my own, and I couldn't hack it. I rang the airport, booked a flight back and went home without telling Manchester United. They didn't take too kindly to it.

'Then Johnny Giles had just got the manager's job at West Brom and I went over to Albion and never thought anything of it. I'm not racial [sic], I mean, but I'd never seen a black person in my life 'til I'd gone to Birmingham. It was funny, they were all wearing tea cosies and carrying ghetto blasters and I thought, "What's going on?" I'd only been over in Ireland for four days and that was when he arrived at the house.

'He took three of us from the same club. I think basically he did it because he knew what it was like as a young lad going away himself and trying to settle on your own. So he brought three of us. It helped to a degree, but the first years were awful. I suffered terrible with homesickness. To be fair to West Brom and to Johnny Giles, he used to send us home every six weeks for a long weekend. I would play on the Saturday, went home on the Saturday night and came back on Tuesday night, direct to training on the Wednesday. So I used to go home and I would stay longer and longer.

'It got to the stage where my dad sat down with us and said, "Look, if you want to come home, come home. You've got to make a choice. If it's what you want to do, you've got to stay, and you've got to stop coming home every six weeks." In the end I decided to give it a go, but I didn't like Birmingham and I couldn't settle there. As I say, the first three or four years, the homesickness was a terrible thing. Sundays, I dreaded Sundays because you didn't train and it was the longest day of the week. When you were an apprentice then, you used to have to be in at eight in the morning. You cleaned boots, you'd brush out the stands, you'd paint the stands, your mind was always active and it made the day longer. So you were always doing something during the week, but Sunday was harder. I went home one summer and I said to my dad, "I don't want to go back". He said, "That's fine, fair enough, that's grand."

'The next minute Nobby Stiles arrived. He was then manager of Preston. He was also Johnny Giles' brother-in-law. Gilesie had left West Brom by this stage. Ronnie Allen was the manager who came in the interim; great player for West Brom in the late 50s or early 60s, I think it was. Then Ron Atkinson got the job. I had no problems with Ron at all; it was the fact that I couldn't settle in Birmingham. And he was as good as gold. They offered us a new contract, my old contract was up, so they offered us a new one, but I didn't want to sign it.

'It takes me to the point of signing my first contract, my first professional contract at West Brom. I walked in and it was the secretary in those days. Obviously, being a young pro, there were no wages or anything like that involved. They said, "We are going to offer you a two years professional contract." I thought it was great, that it was brilliant. They got the contract out and said, "You need to sign there, there and there." I looked at it and it was blank. They said, "Don't worry about it, just sign there and there, and we'll put the figures in later." When I was an apprentice at West Brom I was on £6 a week in my first year and you got your digs paid for. And as I've already said, they'd pay for you to fly home every six weeks. The second year I was on £8 a week and you weren't taxed on that, so it was all money in your pocket. So, being naïve then, I just signed the contract. I was getting £45 pounds a week. By the time I'd paid my tax and my digs, I ended up being £2 a week worse off than when I was an apprentice. Then if I wanted to go home, I had to pay for that myself as well.

'So Nobby came over and said, "Look, just come and train with us, come and do pre-season training." I went to Preston and it was a great club, lovely people and Nobby Stiles was a great lad. Alan Kelly, who I've already mentioned, played there for a lot of years in goal, he was his assistant. I liked it and one thing another, then they offered us a two years contract. It went to a tribunal; they couldn't agree a fee. Nobby had said, "We're prepared to go to £70,000", and if I'd known then what I know now, I would have said, "Give me the other £20,000", because they got us for £50,000. £20,000 was an awful lot of money in 1979.

'When you'd seen Nobby Stiles playing, you'd thought that he was hard and would have kicked you, and he was that type of player. We used to play this big game, everybody at the club played it on a Monday – it was just a loosener. If Nobby had fallen out with you, you always knew when he was going to kick you because he took his glasses off. That way he claimed that he'd never seen you. It's true what they say about him that he couldn't see because he'd come in and he would have a black shoe and a brown shoe on. Or he'd have odd coloured socks on. But he was the most nervous individual I'd ever met. He used to be physically sick before games when he was manager because of the pressure, but he was a great fella. We had a reasonable season, but the following season things didn't go well and Nobby got sacked.

'Then Tommy Docherty came in and the Doc thought he was still at Manchester United. He was throwing money around like there was no tomorrow. He didn't last long. Then a well-known former Newcastle manager came in, Gordon Lee, and I didn't hit it off with Gordon at all. Geoff Nulty was his assistant and I didn't like him either. Gordon was a very arrogant, self-opinionated individual who I didn't see eye-to-eye with at all. And he gave me a free transfer. In fact, there was another lad, Stevie Doyle, who came with me, who actually ended up at Sunderland and won a Third Division championship medal.

'Alan Kelly, who keeps cropping up, rang me because Tommy Docherty had then since moved to Australia to manage a team over there. They had rung us and said, "Do you want to come out here?" I thought, "England is far enough from home, you know, Australia's a long way away." Anyway, Alan rang us and said, "Look, I know Arthur Cox. Will you go up? He wants you and Doyley to go up." Arthur Cox had been assistant to old Alan Ball at Preston when Alan Kelly was in goal. Well, we came up and my first thoughts were "Newcastle, no" because every time I played here it was raining, it was dark, it was dull, it was horrible. To be fair, first impressions, you know, because I always thought it was dark and gloomy. Everywhere looked dark and grey. We came up and we trained and played games, and one thing and another, and I've been here ever since, basically. So it couldn't have been that dark and gloomy.'

John can be found at all Newcastle United games, home and away, because of his local radio work. I asked him for his thoughts on the changes to St James' Park.

'It's amazing how in 20 years, just over 20 years, the stadium has changed. I mean, the old West Stand, it wasn't the Milburn Stand then, it was just a big wooden shack with the press room at the top; it was like a semi-circle. When you played reserve games, that's where Arthur Cox used to go and you could hear him bellowing at you. And you would go "Oh no, he's here again". But the two ends, they were both uncovered. Obviously they built the East Stand and they were supposed to take it around the Leazes End, but they ran out of money, which was nothing new for Newcastle United in those days. The Gallowgate, there was always a good atmosphere. Even though they're getting 52,000 now, the season that we got promoted, '83–84, there was 32–34,000, and I still think there was more noise then.

'I think that a lot of it is down to the all-seating as well. I agree that it had to be done for safety reasons, but I think that when there were terraces the atmosphere was just so much better. People wanted to be in the same place week in week out, which meant that by half-one, two o'clock, the stadium was half full. You used to play and you knew exactly where people were, especially people who gave you abuse. You used to run out and think, you'd look to the same spot and you go, "Oh no, he's there again. He's here every week." The stadium, it's one of the best in the country now, without a doubt. It's a little bit misshapen, I think, because of the East Stand. If they could get the East Stand in line with the rest of it, it would be an unbelievable stadium, but they can't.'

Newcastle United have a purpose-built training facility nowadays. John looked back on his training days and recalled a well-known refreshing character from the past.

'We used to train at Benwell and there was a gym in it, a fair-sized gym, that we used to use. And we had a weight room with a multigym in it. I go to the new training ground now and I have to have a little smirk because of this multigym that we had. Everybody remembers Ronnie at Benwell. Ronnie was an elderly gentleman who walked with a bit of limp. He was brilliant and he made the best tea in the world. He made this huge silver teapot. It was always there waiting for you when you came in. Ronnie was brilliant. His daughter worked at the ground for a while. He was a lovely fella. I think that's a little sad about the modern game, the fact that there are no characters like that left any more. There is no one that you can really associate with. I don't think that togetherness is there. I suppose that it's progress as well because the club has got so big now. I suppose that these things had to happen. But I still think it's a little bit sad.'

Over the decades there have been a variety of pre-match routines reported by former players, some more interesting and successful than others. John's recollections of matchday routines certainly illustrate this.

'The year that we got promoted we used to go to the Swallow Hotel before our home games. We used to meet there for pre-match and I hated it. I used to prefer to be able to do my own thing. No, we didn't do it the year we got promoted, we did it the previous years and I used to hate it. I'd sooner have a lie-in, get up, have a bit to eat, walk up and get a paper, come back, then just arrive at the ground for one o'clock, half-one. But Arthur [Cox] had this thing – it was so boring 'cause you were always trying to kill time. Then you used to be there from half-10, 11 o'clock, just killing time.

'The promotion season, he changed it; we just used to meet at the ground. I remember, all that promotion season, I wore the same shirt, same socks, same underpants, same tie, same jacket, same trousers, same shoes. Everything was exactly the same for home games. By the end of the season the shirt collar was all frayed, the cuffs were all frayed, the tie had stains on it, the socks had holes in them, the underpants were worn to a cinder, there was no thread in them, in fact the thread had no thread. But that was superstition. I was always out last, always the last one out. I put my left boot on last as well. It's a stupid thing, but it's a habit-forming thing, you know. It's like everything, once you get into the habit of doing it, you can't get out of it.

'That promotion season, I actually only missed one game. I got dropped at Derby and we were 2–0 up at half-time; John Trewick played right-back. We ended up getting beat 3–2. The following week, we were playing Huddersfield at St James' and they were going with the same side. On the Friday night I went out for a couple of drinks 'cause I wasn't involved. The next minute, the phone rings, 10 o'clock, you find out that you're playing, and I'm going, "Oh no, I can't". Even back then, having a drink on a Wednesday, that was it from a personal point of view. We ended up winning 5–2, we beat Huddersfield, and I did alright. I never missed another match. The following Friday, I thought, "Should I go out and have a couple of drinks?" because everything had gone that well. But I ended up not doing it. I've got to admit that the thought did enter my head.'

John made his first appearance for Newcastle United on 1 September 1982, coming on as a substitute away at Blackburn Rovers. It was the first of many games during a memorable two seasons.

'I remember coming on as a sub at Blackburn. I remember my full debut was away at Rotherham. I didn't know I was playing until half-one. John Craggs had come back to the club at the same time as I arrived and he was the number one right-back, but I played against Rotherham away. It was on *Match of the Day* and we beat them 5–1. Kevin Keegan got four and Kevin Todd got the other one. Emlyn Hughes missed a penalty. He was the player-manager for Rotherham. Mick Martin played in midfield, Terry Mac played in front of me. It was brilliant. I think my home debut was against Shrewsbury, I can't recall, but I remember the Rotherham game away.

'The '83–84 season was an unbelievable season. It just seemed to start and then it was finished. It was one of those seasons when you didn't want it to end, you know. You just wanted to keep playing because we had sell-outs, week in week out. People were locked out for the Manchester City game, for Chelsea, Sheffield Wednesday, even for Carlisle because they were flying high when they came. You couldn't get in the stadium; it was full at half-one, a quarter to two. Nowadays the stadium's half-empty five minutes before kick-off. It used to be brilliant, absolutely fabulous. We went to Maine

Road, 42,000, the same at Hillsborough. We went to Chelsea and got absolutely murdered; they beat us 4–0. Arthur then brought Glenn Roeder in; he was a great lad, a good leader. They were just tremendous games, unbelievable games. The Manchester City game away, we beat them 2–1; a fabulous game. Again, the performance here against City, when we beat them 5–0; Peter Beardsley got a hat-trick. We beat Carlisle here 5–1, drew with Chelsea, lost to Sheffield Wednesday when we really battered them and shouldn't have lost.

'The real disappointment of that season was going to Cambridge, who hadn't won for a record 20-odd games or so. If we'd won, we were almost guaranteed promotion, and we got beat 1–0. One of our supporters came into the dressing room afterwards, busted into the dressing room, crying his eyes out. He says, "You'd better put it right against Derby." Of course we beat Derby 4–0 – another great team performance. Then the last day of the season, we really wrapped it up against Brighton. Of course Kevin scored as well.

'It was really the inspiration of bringing Kevin in, I suppose. But my argument is that Kevin Keegan would never have come here if I hadn't signed a couple of weeks earlier. I tell everybody that the chairman told Kevin, "You've got to come to Newcastle because I've just signed John Anderson." Both as a player and when he came back as a manager, Kevin was an inspiration. I was in the RVI having my last operation, an ankle operation, on the day that Kevin became manager. I'd just woken up, just come round, and the sports news was on the radio. I was heartbroken really because, having played with him as a player, I knew what he was like. To play for him would have been unbelievable. He got the best out of people. He made average players into good players and good players into very good players. He got the best out of Peter Beardsley, Chris Waddle – not that they weren't great players in their own right anyway. I think that he made them believe that they were truly great players. He installed self-belief in everybody in the side really. So to miss out on playing for him, that was a major disappointment.'

Following promotion to the old First Division, Newcastle United were subsequently relegated at the end of the 1988–89 season. The opportunity to bounce straight back was denied by arch-rivals Sunderland in a play-off semi-final over two legs in May 1990. John recalled what a difficult period it was.

'Well, the play-offs against Sunderland were heartbreak, but the season before was probably the hardest season I've ever had. That was the season of the supporters wanting change. You were going out playing and there was "sack the board", this out, that out. You were going out for warm-ups and you were getting booed. You were getting booed even before the game had kicked off. I've seen a seasoned international, Kenny Sansom, going out for a warm-up, coming to the end of the tunnel and going, "I don't need this, it's not right." I went, "You want to see them when they really get angry."

'Jim Smith, who I had a lot of time for and a lot of respect for, was a man's man. When you needed a kick up the backside, he gave you one. When you needed an arm around you, he'd give you that as well. But whatever he said inside four walls stayed inside four walls. I had an awful lot of respect for him, a great guy. He was unlucky at the time that he was here, as I say, with everything that was going on. Sir John Hall was coming in, everybody else was going out. There was pressure on everybody, pressure to perform. It was very difficult to play under the circumstances with everything that was going on. But losing to Sunderland, I probably felt it more than a lot of the lads as I'd been here a lot longer than they had. And I knew what it really meant to the supporters to lose to Sunderland. Having gone to Roker Park and played so well, and probably should have won the game, only coming away 0–0. We didn't do ourselves justice on the Wednesday night; we didn't play well. We just didn't perform and that was from one to 11. We just let everybody down, which was a major disappointment.'

During his career with Newcastle United, John scored 15 goals, but one in particular stood out.

'The one that always springs to mind is the goal at Leeds in the promotion season because that was the one that got us up and running. It was the first game of the season away at Leeds. I always enjoyed playing at Leeds. For some reason I always seemed to do well at Leeds. It wasn't the cleanest of strikes in the world. What was the one that I remember the most? I remember the free-kick at Watford. Kevin Brock touched it to me and it flew in the top right-hand corner. But the two that I remember the most are probably the one at Leeds and the one at home to Millwall on the second last day of the season that we got relegated. From 20 yards, I hit it full on the volley and the majority of the crowd, 14,000 of them, missed it because they were watching Mirandinha. I got a decent one at Hull as well, a decent strike, but I didn't score enough to forget too many.'

As a defender John faced some tough opponents, but he recalled the day that he received some words of wisdom from an old master.

'Leeds, funnily enough, keep cropping up. Arthur Graham was playing at outside-left for Leeds. He was a good player; he was a Scottish international. It was the opening day of the season again and Joe Harvey always used to come with us. Joe was a lovely man. Anyway, I'm prancing about and he comes and sits down. He says, "You don't look relaxed, son. Are you worried about this fella?" I said, "Yeah, I am a little bit, to be fair." Joe says, "Well, just see how quick he can limp around the halfway line." So they won the toss, kicked off, and I went straight to him and I hit him just around chest height. Joe was there with a fag in his mouth and he gave me the thumbs up. I never saw Arthur Graham again. Mark Hughes was always a handful as were Dalglish and Rush from the great Liverpool side. And Wimbledon were horrible to play against because they just battered you. John Fashanu was just nasty and dirty. The lad Vinnie Jones just tried to be a bully but he wasn't really.'

John settled in the North East after he finished playing for Newcastle United and through his local radio work still has regular contact with the Toon Army. He has shared a good relationship with the supporters but it was a slow start.

'The supporters, I've got to admit, when I first came I had a hard time with the supporters. I'd like to think I'd won them over. In the end they were great with me after 10 years. The thing about supporters is that you're never going to keep them all happy. Some of them will like you and some of them are not going to like you;

it doesn't matter what you do or how you play. You're not going to be their cup of tea. But overall the supporters were first class. And it's true what they say, they're knowledgeable, they know their football up here. If you're honest with them, they'll be okay with you. If you were having a bad time, but you were trying to put it right and you were giving them 100 percent, they would stick with you. It's when it's not going right for you and you start going missing, they would get on your back. But they are great supporters and it would be lovely to think that with Graeme Souness they could actually win something. They do deserve some silverware and it would be nice if it did happen.'

Not surprisingly, having played for Newcastle United for 10 years, John experienced a number of managerial changes during his career.

'I've got a lot of thoughts on managers. Arthur Cox, it was a love-hate relationship. It was only after Arthur had gone that I realised how much he had done for us. And he knew how to get the best out of us and he knew how to go about doing that. When I think back to the Liverpool cup game on the Friday – I think it was one of the first televised games – Liverpool beat us 4–0. We were going well in the old Second Division. They had Souness, Rush, Lawrenson, Hansen. It was a game that afterwards Kevin [Keegan] decided that he was going to chuck it because Mark Lawrenson had given him five yards and caught up with him.

'Afterwards, we came back and we were at Benwell. Arthur Cox said, "I want to see you." I thought to myself, "What does he want?" I walked in and he had a seat with the legs cut off so that you were lower down and were looking up at him. So he had his feet up on the desk, looking out of the window, and he said, "Have you seen the match?" I went, "No I haven't seen it." He said, "Did you tape it?" I said, "Yeah, but I don't think I want to watch it." He said, "Well, go and watch it." I came back the next day and he was waiting for me. He was always the first in anyway.

He said, "Did you watch it? What did you think?" I said, "They played very well. They're a good side, worked hard, passed it well. We worked hard but didn't pass it well." Arthur said, "Did you notice anything?" I said, "Like what?" He went, "We were that bad, you were our best player. Now you can go." He just knew how to wind us up.

'As I've already mentioned, Jim Smith was great. A lot of players didn't like him, but I did. Jack Charlton, well Jack was Jack. He would rather have been out fishing or shooting. Malcolm Brown and John Ryan were brought in by Arthur to replace Kenny Wharton and myself. Unfortunately Malcolm did his Achilles at pre-season – unlucky for him but fortunately for me that promotion season. When Jack came in, he called me in and said, "Look, I know you played the majority of games last season, you only missed one game, but you won't be starting. It doesn't matter how pre-season goes." I said, "What are you on about?" He said, "This ******* club can't afford to pay £100,000 for somebody they're not playing." They were his exact words. Malcolm was starting one way or the other. So I was on the bench for the first couple of games. Jack had moved us into centre-back, which I didn't mind.

'Anyway we were at Benwell this day and it was ankle deep in mud. Jack had the centre-backs knocking the ball to the full-backs. So Kenny knocked it to Malcolm and he scuffed it. He couldn't get the ball airborne at all. Jack was in his suit, full jacket and trousers, up to his neck in it. He knocked Malcolm out of the way. Glenn Roeder knocked the ball to him and he hit it up in the air, a good strike of the ball. He said, "Do you think you could do that?" Malcolm caught the ball, he did it again, and he scuffed it. So Jack went and stood about 10 yards away from him and said, "Look, all I want you to do is knock it straight over the top of my head." So Glenn passed to Malcolm who took a run at this ball and hit it. It didn't go above waist height. It hit Jack full in the…he's on his hands and knees in all the mud and that was it, training session was abandoned.

'But Jack came in and he tried to change the way we played. We had played a certain way to get promotion and he felt that we would've gone straight back down with the players that we had. He honestly thought that we weren't good enough. So he changed it, he brought two big lads in: Tony Cunningham and George Reilly. We knocked it long and played off them. It wasn't great to watch and it wasn't great to play. Jack's argument was, if you're not prepared to do it this way, I'll get somebody who is. So you learned his way. I've got to say, at international level he was superb, but I don't think he wanted to be involved in the day-to-day running of the football club.

'Willie McFaul was a lovely man. Willie was first-team coach to Arthur Cox and obviously first-team coach to Jack as well. He was a great fella but he was too nice. I remember when he got the job, he called in the senior boys – there was Glenn, Kenny, Davey Mac, me – and he said, "Look, I've got the job on a temporary basis. If you boys could get me the job on a permanent basis, I'll look after you." We did well, we did great, we finished eighth, had a good season. Then he brought in John Hendrie, Andy Thorn, John Robertson and Peter Jackson. All of a sudden these guys are driving around in club cars, it had never been heard of before, and that was when it all went wrong. He forgot about the boys who'd got him the job and he brought these new lads in, big money, gave them cars, and there was a lot of resentment there. Funnily enough, when he did eventually get the sack, it was the same four senior players who went to see him. He said, "I know I've made mistakes and it's cost us."

'I'd rather not talk about Ossie Ardiles. He was great with the young lads. When I was injured and was told that my career was over, he never asked how I was doing or what I'd been told. Derek Wright, the physio, was great; he was a different class. Ossie would say things to you and you knew that as soon as you'd walked out he would be calling you, saying something different. He would always say to you what he thought you wanted to hear instead of being honest. I didn't like the man. We very rarely spoke.'

John remains close to Newcastle United through local radio and he always tries to keep his comments as honest as possible without rocking the boat.

'The thing about it is that you've got to be diplomatic because you want to say things, but you don't want to upset players. You don't want to say the wrong things because you think about when you were in their shoes and people were saying things like that. So you do try to be diplomatic and comment on it being a team situation rather than an individual one. I know when I played I didn't like being singled out. It does happen now like it happened then, but it wasn't nice.'

Finally, returning to memories of his own childhood, John told me a great story about a recent trip back home. He had been on a family visit to Ireland and he was watching some small boys playing football in the street. It was just like the old days. The temptation was too great.

'There was this group of little lads, you know the sort, snotty noses, kicking this ball around. Well, I couldn't stop myself and I joined in the kick-about. One of the lads looked at me quizzically and said, "Didn't you used to be John Anderson?" I thought that was brilliant.'

Chapter 11

BILLY WHITEHURST
(1985–86)

WILLIAM WHITEHURST was born in Thurnscoe, near Barnsley, on 10 June 1959. Signed from Hull City in December 1985 for £232,500, Billy was a centre-forward at St James' Park, making 30 senior starts for Newcastle United and scoring seven goals. Like most players from his era, Billy was soon kicking a ball, but his football career did not immediately take off when he finished his education.

'I started off like most young lads at school, playing in the school team. I just went through every year from junior school, from say like eight years old: they had teams all the way up to leaving school. When I left school I was a bit disenchanted with football, when I was about 15, and I didn't play again until I was 18. I had three years away from it and got into the greyhound scene instead. Then, when I was 18, I went to play for a pub side. I started playing for a pub team at the Butchers Arms at Thurnscoe, where I come from. I had a season playing for them. I went from there to Mexborough Town in the old Midland League, which would be like the Unibond League now, or something like that. Then I started getting paid for it, like, say 20 quid a week or whatever.

'Then Hull City asked me to go and have a game in the reserves for them. They had seen me playing in a Midland League select side against Nottingham Forest and they asked me to play for a trial in a game for Hull City reserves against Notts County reserves. They just signed me on from there. It was a good era, that. I know when I went to Hull in 1980, they were getting bigger crowds then than they are now. You would like to see them in the top flight because they've never been in the top flight. They've got the facilities there now. Obviously it's the same as everywhere else. Most football crowds are fickle – they will support winning teams. But if Hull City ever achieve that status and get into the Premier League, they will fill the place.'

When Billy was growing up in his native Yorkshire in the 1960s and early 1970s, the famous Busby Babes influenced his early memories of football.

'I think the first football match that I went to was Sheffield United against Manchester United and I think George Best scored, but he wasn't particularly my hero. It was more Bobby Charlton. More so, I liked playing football rather than watching it. So I didn't really get involved with going and watching players. But Manchester United always seemed to be big in those days. They were brought to the public eye with the Munich Air Disaster and I think that is why they have got the biggest support in the world. What is it that they say in the Guinness advert? About 99% of Manchester United supporters have never been to Manchester. Bobby Charlton, I always thought was brilliant; I still do to be fair. When they show some of the old footage on television, he was a fantastic player. And he's a North East man, isn't he?'

When Billy moved to Boothferry Park in 1980 to play for my home-town club, Hull City, he found that becoming a professional footballer was a bit different to what he had been used to.

'It was a shock to the system, going from non-League to League football. Obviously, to be fair, you always think that you are fit, and you think that you are this, that and the other. But when I got there, I found I wasn't as fit as others there. Your first touch is all-important in professional football; well my second touch was 'tackle'. So it was really a couple of years before I settled down and started playing and doing alright, like. Then, when I settled in at Hull, we had a bit of success. We got a couple of promotions in three seasons. We got promotion, just missed out on promotion on goal difference and then got promotion the following season. The season after that we were about fifth in the League in the old Second Division. Then I got sold to Newcastle, which, to be fair, we were a bit…I don't know what the word is. I think that if I had stayed…well, not just me, they sold a few players at that particular time. If they had kept me and a couple of players who they had let go, and brought a couple of players in, then Hull could have got promotion that year. That would have meant they'd have gone up into the top flight. But it wasn't to be. I went to Newcastle and I was their record signing at the time.'

Billy signed for Newcastle United in December 1985 from Hull City. I asked him about how he found out about the move.

'Joe Harvey had come to watch me play against Manchester City. We played them at Hull in the League Cup. I don't know what round it was. Joe came down and he was doing a bit of scouting for Newcastle. The first thing that I knew about it, Don Robinson phoned me up and asked me to come to the ground. He just told me that Newcastle had put in a bid for me and they had accepted it. It was up to me whether I wanted to go or not. I found it a bit strange that they were letting me go at a time when they looked as though they could get promotion to the top flight for the first time. But they had obviously made up their minds that they wanted rid of me. Well it was not so much that they wanted rid of me, they didn't want to stand in my way if I wanted to go. So I decided that I would like to go. It was a big honour for me. I mean, Newcastle are one of the biggest teams in the country, aren't they?

'They've been going through a bit of turmoil recently, a bit of a rough patch. Let's be honest, if you are playing for a team like Newcastle United, you should be proud to put on the shirt, wherever you are playing, shouldn't you? When players start dictating to managers where they want to play, there is something wrong. I felt a bit for Bobby Robson. To be fair, that ****** Bellamy, Bobby should have ****** him off in my eyes when he was in charge. It was similar with Dyer when he refused to play in a certain position. Then you had what Dyer and Bowyer did. I just find it hard to digest; I think it's scandalous.'

Billy had a reputation for being a hard man on the pitch and, if you believe the rumours, off the pitch as well. He fondly remembers his playing days with Sheffield United and the motivating style of manager Dave 'Harry' Bassett.

'He's one of those managers who is a motivator, if you like. His classic words to me when he sent me on as a sub were, "Go and cause some ********, big man". That's Harry's style, isn't it? Obviously all managers are different. You get some managers who don't want anything to do with the physical side of it. They just want to get it down and pass it. Harry liked people to get stuck in and get the other team on the back foot kind of thing. That's what his style was. To be fair, if you look at his record, he brought success throughout his career as a manager. I would imagine there aren't many managers about, in the past or now, who've got as good a record as Harry, simply with promotions. Wimbledon and Sheffield United were teams that he did tremendous with. Who's to say that it didn't work? I think they've all got their good points. Then sometimes you get an exceptional manager like such as Alex Ferguson at the moment who has won everything.

'I was just a bread-and-butter centre-forward; someone they used to call "an old-fashioned centre-forward". Playing where I played, I don't think I would last long today. I don't think I would get through six games without being suspended. It was a bit more rough and tumble when I played. Mind you, I only stopped in 1993 at Crewe. They've got cameras now; they've got cameras all over. Wherever you are on the pitch, they've got a camera on you. They're on you for 90 minutes. I just can't understand players now who are diving in the penalty area. There was one the other day; he went down as though he'd been shot. Nobody touched him but he went down. Players nowadays know the cameras are on them, so it makes them look stupid. They're diving or faking as though they've been head-butted, they're going down and rolling about, getting a fellow pro sent off. All it does, the camera will focus on the incident. To stop that, if they got a red card, I very much doubt that they would do it again. I just can't understand how players can do it, knowing that the cameras are on them.

'Myself, if I got injured, I stayed down, because I was injured. If you look at foreign players in England, your continental players, you see them rolling about, which we've always known about. When they come here and they've played for a couple of months, you find that they get into our way of thinking type thing. You see a bit of it, but not as much as they would do like in Italy. If they get tackled in an Italian game, they roll over about three million times, don't they? They look as though they've been shot. When I was injured, I stayed on the floor. As I say, I was just a run-of-the-mill centre-forward. I grafted hard, I always liked training and I always gave 110 percent. I put myself about. That was basically me. The thing is, it's frowned upon big style now because you could kill someone. It was a case of the centre-half was out to get you. There were no cameras. Nowadays, if you'd been watching a game against Sheffield United, Hull City or Wigan, if you hit somebody off the ball, you might think that you've got away with it. But you wouldn't get away with it because the next week the FA would look at the footage.

'When we were playing, you were getting smashed into the corners. The first bother from a centre-half, he would come and give you one in the kidneys. It was a case of this was what you were going to get that day. You reacted by giving him a bit back. Elbows were flying all over the place. Hence the expression "Put a boot on his elbow" or "Put a boot on his head". There was more going off with elbows. What I'm trying to say is it was a lot more physical then. They've tightened up on the tackles from behind and things like that now. I think to a certain extent that it's not been all that good for the game. At that time a lot of supporters just went to watch for the confrontation between the centre-forward and the centre-half. It was part of the game that some people liked. Nowadays that sort of thing has been all taken away. The first sign of anything physical, it's the whistle. I think a lot of the time in matches today it is stop-start more than it's ever been. There doesn't seem to be that flow like there used to be. At the end of the day it's still a man's game. There's got to be some contact.

'I sometimes think that the ref thinks you've gone to watch him. That's another thing from my time; you had some good refs about. They would talk to you. They would pull you to one side and say, "******* hell, Billy, what are you playing at? What's going off?" You could relate to them. I used to do some things that you wouldn't do now. I was playing for Sheffield United and we'd played against

Crystal Palace. They had an assistant manager to Coppell and Harry said to me after the game that he'd been slagging me off for when I was at Reading. So I went into their dressing room, grabbed him by the throat and I squeezed his ******* throat. They all ****** sat down and they wouldn't come near me.'

First impressions are often very important and Billy vividly recalled his introduction to life with Newcastle United.

'When I got there, I went up on the train, Joe Harvey came and picked me up and we went straight to the ground. I think they were like in old Portakabins then. We did us talking there, like. I remember just the first day we got there. I'd gone in and talked to Willie [McFaul] about football. It seemed from his words that he'd been trying to get me for a long while, which I didn't know about. His words were, "Pleased to get you here after all this time." So it seemed as though it had gone on for a while for him and he was pleased to get me there. We had a chat about contracts and what have you, and we agreed terms. Agents were just starting to come in. I didn't have an agent. They were just starting to come in, not like they are now. They're parasites now. I think that's another thing about football. I know they've all got a job to do, but they seem to be getting more money than brain surgeons.

'Then, after we'd done the business at the ground, I remember Willie taking me to a hotel in Jesmond, the Imperial, and he put me there. He just said, "I'll introduce you to someone". John Bailey was staying there. He phoned his room number, but unfortunately he wasn't in his room, he was at the bar. And that's where we stayed for the rest of my short career at Newcastle. I think that introducing me to Bails at that particular stage in my Newcastle career wasn't the wisest thing to do for me or John. So it went downhill from there.

'My debut at home was against Southampton. I can remember that day; it was fantastic. Not knocking Hull City in any way, they were fantastic supporters there and I had great support there, but

Newcastle supporters were great that day, and it was just a normal home game. I've never been at Wembley so I had nothing to compare it with. I've only ever seen the FA Cup on the telly. But coming down that tunnel at St James' Park, it was tremendous. It was one of them days in your life, few and far between, when the hairs stick up on the back of your neck. It were just fantastic. I'll never forget that day. Training was at Benwell. I was manager at Frickley in the Unibond League and Newcastle had more people watching them train. That was always quite an experience. You'd had a good few hundred just watching training up at Benwell and it were enjoyable. I always thought it were good. The players seemed to get on well enough.'

Billy got off to a slow start at Newcastle but had nothing but praise for the majority of the supporters. His career was to sadly turn sour due to the actions of a small group of supporters and his very public response to them when he stuck two fingers up to them.

'I'm sure that they thought, "What have we got here?" Towards the end of the season I started scoring a few goals and I started playing better. They were fantastic in respect that they probably thought that I wasn't good enough for what they wanted. But they saw that I gave 100 percent and that goes a long way with Newcastle supporters. They know if they've got someone there who's giving everything for the cause and they don't suffer fools gladly. You can have someone who has a lot of talent, but they don't put the effort in. They would sooner have somebody with not so much talent who is going sweat a bit of blood for the club. That's my opinion of them and that sums them up. When you think about it, when I went there, contrary to most people's beliefs and thoughts, the supporters were absolutely brilliant. I mean, I didn't score for 11 games.

'They've got that cherished number nine shirt, haven't they? You know, you're bought to score goals. They're probably looking for cultured players. They had Gascoigne and Beardsley, who at the time were two of the best players in Europe, never mind this country. Like in Gascoigne, he's been one of the best players this country's produced in the last ******* 50 years. The crowd's expectations are high and quite rightly so. You know yourself, they go week in week out. It's like a religion to them. I think that they deserve the best and obviously they expect the best. To me personally, I think they were fantastic. They were absolutely great with me and I was quite surprised. I can remember after a few home games, I sat down with Jackie Milburn. He would take me through a few things, what he thought I should do. He was an absolute gentleman. He said, "Billy, you know me, I went through a spell, a dry spell, when I couldn't score a goal. I came to the conclusion that I was just going to shoot instead of laying things off and passing. Just have a try and it might go in for you." He was fantastic. He gave me a lot of encouragement. It was nice that he found the time to sit down and have a chat. He was a legend. He was a really fantastic fella.

'You look at people and you've read about them when you've gone up there, and you think, "What are they going to be like?" Jackie Milburn was absolutely tremendous. Joe Harvey was just the same. What a great bloke. He always had 10 minutes for you, always had a smile on his face and always had a nice word to say. Whatever mood you were in, he could always get you happy and thinking, "It's nice to be here". He was just great.

'The incident that caused my downfall, it was all blown out of proportion. It was the second leg of the League Cup, we were losing 2–0 from the first leg and it was 1–0 on the night, so we were 2–1 down to Bradford City. As I was brought off, I got spat at from a few people and my head went. I went back out and I flagged these few people, something which was well-documented. But it was just a rush of blood. You can imagine, can't you? Getting spat at, spit all over my face, it was just disgusting. But it was an absolute minority, you know, but it came across that I was doing it to the majority, which was a load of ********. The majority of Newcastle fans were fantastic with me.

'I thought that Willie [McFaul], who was manager, was a great bloke. I liked him apart from when he told me that he was bombing me out and he was fining me a week's wages for that incident. I told him that he shouldn't fine me a week's wages and that was the beginning of the end. He said, "I can't play you for Newcastle again after what you've done." I told him what had happened, but that didn't really come into the equation. It was a case of, "So what, they spit at you", more or less. It was only a minority but it's still not a very nice thing, is it? It turned it a bit sour, really, what should have been a memorable period of my life, which it was. But it did turn it a bit sour for me. But apart from that, everything else was sweet, with lovely memories. There were some good lads there as well.'

As far as Billy was and still is concerned, his actions were totally misunderstood and were blown out of proportion at the time. Regrettably it was to seal his fate at St James' Park and he was soon on his way to Oxford. Life as a professional footballer has changed significantly since Billy played and he reflected on these changes.

'I was talking to someone today about it. How can you afford it with a family of two or three kids? The fans are seeing the extortionate amount of money the players are on. You look at football as an entertainment. They are entertainers like the Spice Girls were supposed to be. They are millionaires, the Spice Girls, they can't sing a note but they are millionaires for entertaining. So I can't knock footballers, but when you look at lads who are working day in and day out, they have to pay those prices. For a footballer it is like winning the pools every week.

'If you were getting £70–80,000 a week and you were wanting to dictate where you played, or you won't put the shirt on and sweat a bit of blood, you can understand why the fans get frustrated. You at least want to see players who want to play for your team. You only need to look at what's going off and you see that the fans are paying good money. If you've got a family, it's a lot of money. When you look at the papers, you see how much the players are on. Let's be fair, the players can't live in a bubble. They've got to go out and enjoy themselves, but at the end of the day you can see how people get frustrated.'

It was inevitable that a player of Billy's character would have collected a catalogue of stories from his playing days. Unfortunately many of these cannot be made public. I did manage to salvage one or two.

'I remember the time when Willie had quite a few injuries and it was getting his hair off, and he was getting a bit frustrated. The team had had a couple of bad results. He'd got Gascoigne injured and quite a few of his first team. It was getting him down a bit and it had just been in the paper that Peter Beardsley's wages had gone to £2,000 a week. I'd gone to training and got out of my car. Willie's walking by and he says, "Alright Billy?" I said, "Yeah, not bad, but Peter's not feeling two grand." He went, "Oh my god, not another one." I just walked past him and laughed. The penny finally dropped. The last thing he needed at the time was Peter being bad.

'This one was one of the classic stories of all time. John Bailey was in the bath after we'd been training. There was John Bailey, Glenn Roeder – 'Captain Kirk' as we used to call him – Peter Beardsley, Paul Gascoigne, Joe Allon and me, all of us soaking away. Joe says, "Bails, got any stuff?" John Bailey says, "Yeah, there's some shampoo in my toilet bag." So, he'd gone to Bails' toilet bag and he says, "Bails, you've got a European Cup medal, a League Championship medal and an FA Cup medal in your toilet bag." John says, "**** me, I wondered where they'd gone, kid." He just winked at Peter Beardsley, who'd won nothing at that time. Then me and Bails got up and went for a shandy. That was all you got out of Bails, "Tell me we are going for a shandy, big man." We had some good times.

'I also remember David McCreery; he was another great bloke. Week in week out, you would get David playing, but the headlines would always be "Will McCreery make it?" because he never trained through the week. The headlines in the *Evening Chronicle* on a Friday would be "Will McCreery be fit for Saturday?" He was always fit. I can remember one day when we were playing away. He roomed with the big Greek god, Jeff Clarke. Jeff had got some flu or something. Well, David was always a bit of a hypochondriac. Jeff had got his Benylin or whatever it was on the side of the bed. When Jeff woke up the next morning, David's supped it. David says, "I thought you wouldn't mind, Jeff." They were a great set of lads and I really did have some good times.'

Billy was a colourful character on the football pitch and remains just as colourful off it today. He was not always the most subtle of players, but he was a centre-forward who gave maximum effort, no matter which team he was playing for. Looking back to the incident that hastened his departure from St James' Park, it could be argued that it was that small minority of Newcastle fans who spat in his face who were responsible for his ultimate downfall. For that reason, it is difficult not to have some sympathy for Billy, who really did just want to do well at Newcastle. Contrary to popular belief, usually fuelled by the local media, the majority of Newcastle supporters do remember Billy for what he tried to achieve at St James' Park and probably wished that he could have stayed longer. It was recognised that Billy gave everything and there is no doubt that he was the big man who could "go out and cause some ********".

Chapter 12

WARREN BARTON
(1995–2002)

WARREN DEAN BARTON was born on 19 March 1969 in Islington, London. Signed from Wimbledon in June 1995 for a record £4 million, he made 193 senior starts for Newcastle United and scored five goals. Warren gained three full England caps. Like many professional footballers, Warren was kicking a ball with his brother from an early age.

'I think that having an older brother, John, who is four years older than me, he was playing for a team in London that was quite well known in the area, Redbridge United. They were probably like

Wallsend Boys. They had teams from say Under-7s right up to Under-18s. It was an established club, had a good reputation in the area and always had scouts going to look at the games. So it was through my older brother really that I decided to go into football. When we used to play over at the park, we had a full-length pitch and we would play there until it got dark and my mum or dad used to call us in.

'So that's where I think the football side came into it and then I was playing in the school team. If you're not intelligent at school, you've got to be good at sport. Football, being what it was, it was my vice really. They were my first memories of playing and at the time, of course being an Arsenal supporter as well, I was watching games with people like Liam Brady, David O'Leary and Frank Stapleton. They were my first memories of me getting into football at that time. Obviously I would play at the park with my brother but my first experience of getting into a team was at Under-9s. That was the first time that I really got into an organised situation where everybody turned up, everybody wore the same kit, you had half-times and you had officials there. Then it just progressed from there really. You do well in your school team, you play well for your county and then in the South of England at Redbridge United you had scouts coming round to watch you. At the time Watford was the up-and-coming team, with Graham Taylor, coming through all the divisions and playing in the old First Division. They had a scout there called Ken Brooks who had people like David James, Dean Holdsworth and Tim Sherwood. He had that sort of catchment area for bringing people through. At the time as well, I was at Arsenal and Watford up to Under-13s and I had to make a decision. I chose Watford.

'It's funny what people say about agents and advisors. At the time, Watford promised me that I would get a scholarship and would get a first team pro. You took it all as gospel and that was at 12 years of age. That was the sort of future that I was trying to head for. 18 months later I was being told that I was too small, I wasn't going to make it at Watford, and I wasn't right. 18 months earlier I was promised a scholarship and obviously I would be going on to be playing in the first team as a professional. But it was just one of those things. I was fortunate at the time to have my family around me. So they were all behind me and supported me. It's difficult at 13 being told that you're too small and you're not going to be good enough. When Graham Taylor picked me for England, when I was at Wimbledon, he said, "Don't say a word, I know I told you that you were too small, and now I'm picking you for England." It was quite funny in that respect.

'So, I went to Leyton Orient. I went there as a 14 year old and really learned my trade there. To have my opportunity at the time, the government had brought in the old YTS schemes and I was on £22.50 a week, then £27.50 a week in my second year. Yeah, I know, it was "big money" then, and I could start planning for the future. Frank Clark, a local Geordie lad, he was the manager and he said I was too small at the time. He was probably right, I was five foot one and eight and a half stone at 17 years of age. I wasn't exactly going to be pushing people around in the Second Division. Again, that was a difficult time for me. But I ended up playing non-League football for two years with Dagenham and Redbridge. It was literally training at the end of our road. I went down there and had two successful years. And non-League football was probably the best thing for me, because if I had stayed at Orient I would never have got anywhere near the first team. I would have just played reserve-team football. But when you walk into a changing room and you've got firemen, electricians, plumbers and builders in there, you know that if you let in a goal, you will cost them their bonuses. You soon learn to do the right things. That was a great growing up period for me, quite literally in many ways. It's amazing, from the age of 17 to 18, I must have shot up eight or nine inches and put on about two or three stones. I still had a lot to develop as such, but it shows that you get a lot of late developers.'

When Warren was growing up as a child, albeit quite slowly, being a Londoner he supported the biggest local team, Arsenal.

'It was the time when they got to the three cup finals on the trot. It was quite ironic because that's what we were trying to do with Newcastle, with the games against Arsenal, Manchester United and the semi-final against Chelsea. But that was my sort of era. I had obviously heard of Malcolm Macdonald, people like that, but it was Tony Woodcock, Kenny Sansom, that era. But when I was actually playing football at the age of 12 and 13, it was Bryan Robson. He was my idol, if you like. His running style, how he used to play his football was something that I admired. Liam Brady was always a god to me as well. My brother was an Arsenal supporter and my dad went to see some of the games, so that was my first recollection of the football times.'

Warren first came to the attention of Newcastle United long before they bought him. With hindsight they could have saved a lot of money.

'I heard the rumour when I was at Maidstone that they were interested. It was at the time when Ossie Ardiles was in charge, I believe, and Jim Thompson, a Geordie, was the chairman of Maidstone. He had had an offer of £200,000–250,000, but Newcastle weren't prepared to pay that sort of money and they said no. They waited and paid £4 million. I'd been linked with Blackburn and Liverpool at the time, as well as Tottenham, and lo and behold Wimbledon came in and paid £300,000, which was a lot of money to pay for someone from a lower League. In the end it turned out to be a good investment, £300,000 and then five years later selling me off for £4 million. Newcastle could have had the opportunity but then I don't think we would have had the same times with Ossie. It was a different era and a very different time.'

Much was written in the media about Wimbledon during the time that Warren was playing with them. It was inevitable that we would revisit the 'Crazy Gang' era.

'Yes, we speak about it a lot. I think that we are possibly one of the only clubs that have a reunion with the players. The era at the time, there was John Fashanu, Vinnie Jones, Dean Holdsworth, John Scales, Robbie Earle, Marcus Gayle and myself. There are several of us who always go out to dinner, which is quite strange when you think about it, Wimbledon players going out for dinner. But I think that it's just an excuse to go out and have a drink first. But we all get together and normally the club would arrange something. I think that it shows the bond that the players had, playing for Wimbledon at that time with Joe Kinnear. It's only really when you take a step back that you realise how good the squad of players was, and how good the relationship was with the manager. We had good times there. We used to do things to people, to their clothes, cars or whatever. Nowadays you couldn't get away with it. What would happen now is, players would probably sulk, go and tell their agents that they want to leave and won't talk any more. But that's probably what drove us on a lot more. The more people reacted, the more they got upset about it, the more we would do it.

'We would take coach drivers away to Newcastle or wherever it would be across the country, and they would like to wear their best shirt and tie going to St James' Park. We would probably burst into his room about half past 10 at night and take all his clothes and leave him in there. So he would have to wear an old tracksuit or whatever he's been wearing. So we used to do all silly things like that. And Sam Hamman would come down on Monday morning, or before a big game, and he'd want to have a running race across the pitch, and he would have his £1,000 suits and his £250 handmade shoes. We would have running races across the pitch and then trip him up and throw him in the puddles. So it was all a type of bonding and getting together that we used to do. But they were very good times.'

When Warren did sign for Newcastle United, he was the country's most expensive defender and the club's record signing, but not for long.

'Yeah, it was for two days. I'd seen Les Ferdinand two weeks before at a dinner in London and we'd both been spoken to by Arsenal and we were both pencilled in to go there. But George Graham had left and it was before they were bringing in Arsène Wenger, and they didn't have a manager for about seven or eight months. We obviously thought at the time that we were going to Highbury. Newcastle with Sir John [Hall] and Kevin [Keegan] were going out buying quality players at that time. People like Philippe Albert had just come back from the World Cup and they were looking to strengthen again. They went out and got people like Les Ferdinand, David Ginola and Shaka Hislop at the time. Then it just went on from there and the list of players was endless.

'I got a phone call; it was a bank holiday Monday. Newcastle were playing Blackburn and funnily enough Alan Shearer scored at the far post against John Beresford. I had the phone call in the morning and then I had spoken to Kevin and Freddie Fletcher at a hotel in London, and it was all signed and sealed then. But obviously the speculation went on and about six to eight weeks down the line it was all done. I had spoken to Kevin, with all his charisma, and he said, "Come and join a big club." And he wasn't joking. Once I'd spoken to Newcastle, I had no second thoughts at all. I loved every minute of it. Yeah, there was a lot of pressure at the time because, being the record defender and coming up to Newcastle along with Les Ferdinand, the expectations were so high. But the start of that season, the football that we played in the first seven months in particular was fantastic. It was only really the last seven or eight games where it all fell to pieces. I don't know if it will ever be followed. There have been a lot of great players who have come along, but the actual movement and the fluency of football has not been there. For us it was just exciting football.'

During King Kevin's reign at Newcastle United the squad trained at Maiden Castle, Durham. It was quite a crowd puller.

'I had more people watching me train than I had watching me play at Wimbledon in the Premier League games. That was quite intimidating but it was all part of the hype and the culture and the fanaticism of the supporters. You would turn up for training and normally you would get in half an hour beforehand or 45 minutes. We had to be in an hour and a half beforehand. We weren't going to walk past the fans who had been queuing in the snow with their kids wanting things signed. We would all go out there and sign, whether it was Les Ferdinand or one of the reserve team, and you wouldn't come in until you'd signed something. That was the way it always was. It has changed a lot now at the ground, the supporters cannot get near. I think that takes away a lot of the bonding between the fans and the players. That is what this football club is all about. A lot of people say the football club is a community, but I think this place is unique in every way, that it is totally different.

'We used to have people watching us train three or four deep. I remember times when Kevin Keegan and Terry McDermott used to sit on the hamburger stall, having a cup of tea and a sausage roll, watching us train, along with two or three thousand people. They were great times that we had, you know, all the hype, the 12 points lead in the League, and everything was just snowballing along. They were brilliant times. Even the football jersey with the granddad collar style shirt was all part of what was going on.'

Warren had a reputation at the club for being a snappy dresser and his routine on match days really illustrated this fact.

'At home games Peter Beardsley used to pick me up because he lived in Ponteland and I was in Wolsington, and we always used to get in reasonably early. But I'd always used to get up and have my shirt ironed. I would always iron my own shirt; I would do that in the morning. I would have the same breakfast, same routine, go to bed early, have a sleep in the afternoon, the Friday afternoon, and just prepare really. From Wednesday and Thursday you were prepared. Superstitions – I used to have all my clothes laid out. People at the club will tell you about me. I'm very particular about my clothes, how I like everything neat and tidy, and how I used to come to training all smartly dressed. So I used to get my clothes ready for the morning so that all I was concentrating on was getting dressed, having my breakfast and then focusing on the Saturday. I always used to hang the black and white shirt over my clothes until I was ready to go out, whereas some would wear it to warm up in.'

With many of the former players I interviewed, I asked them to highlight key games from their time with Newcastle United. In Warren's case I selected some games that I felt were significant for a variety of reasons. The first game was Newcastle against Liverpool on 10 March 1997 at Anfield. The previous season, when the two teams met in the same fixture, the game ended 4–3 to Liverpool, who won the game in the dying seconds. They said it would never happen again. In his programme notes the then manager of Liverpool Roy Evans wrote, 'It is unlikely that tonight's encounter will provide a spectacle to equal the last occasion Newcastle United visited Anfield.' Although the game did not quite match the previous encounter, it certainly had supporters gripping the edge of their seats. As with the previous game, Liverpool won 4–3 as the dying seconds ticked by.

'It was half the game of the first one, if I'm being totally honest. We were appalling in the first half, 3–0 down at Anfield, with nothing to play for but pride. Then we got ourselves back into the game, with Keith [Gillespie] and Tino [Asprilla] getting a goal each, and I got the equaliser with about one and a half minutes to go. I got into a situation where I won a header, it fell for me in the box, and I just toe-poked it in. I don't actually know what I was doing that far up the pitch. I managed to get it in there. It cost me £250 for kicking a Sky microphone behind the back of the goal. But that was just the adrenalin of the game.

'The only way that I can describe it is like a boxer where you've been knocked down three times and it's the last chance saloon. You end up hitting him and he goes down. That was how it felt, that we had dragged ourselves back into a game where we were dead and buried. I would imagine that a lot of people back home would have turned the telly off at half-time. But we clawed ourselves back into it and, as luck would have it, Robbie Fowler knocked in a header with seconds to go. That was just demoralising. In football sometimes you get what you deserve and probably, looking at the whole picture, that's what we did get. We didn't play particularly well, but we managed to get ourselves back into it. And when you are that close, to lose it, it was a shame.'

The 1997–98 season brought a couple of early encounters with London clubs. On 13 September 1997, Newcastle lost at home 3–1 to Warren's former club, Wimbledon. However he did score the only goal against his former employers. Fortunately for Newcastle United, Warren's eye for goal brought a more satisfactory outcome against Tottenham Hotspur, again at home, on 4 October 1997 with him scoring the winner late in the game. He remembered it well.

'Yes, I scored the winner. There are not too many people who can say that they scored the winner in the 89th minute or whatever it was. There had been a shot on goal and Ian Walker parried it or it got a deflection, and with my left foot I managed to smash it into the roof of the net. I think the pictures in the papers afterwards, of my quite scary facial expressions, showed how much the adrenalin, excitement and passion comes out of your mind and body when you score a winning goal at home for your team, Newcastle United. It was a good time and obviously being an Arsenal fan, a lot of people back home thought that it was special beating Tottenham.'

The third game that I had chosen proved to be a turning point for Warren after a difficult time at St James' Park. It was the game against Crystal Palace at home on 2 January 1999 in the FA Cup third round when Newcastle won 2–1. In his programme notes, manager Ruud Gullit wrote, 'This is a game we are expected to win. Crystal Palace will be well motivated, they know what a fine scalp this is for them.' It was a game in which Warren showed what true commitment really meant.

'Yes, I played at left-back. I think I might be right, but it was the game that changed everybody's opinion at the club. I'd had this good start to the season a couple of years beforehand, then I had a bit of a difficult period. We were down to 10 men, Shay Given got sent off and they had gone 1–0 up. I'd been asked by Ruud to play at left-back, and it was a game where we needed someone to grab it by the scruff of the neck to try and get us back into it. It was one of those games where I just found the energy and Alan [Shearer] scored the crucial goal with a cross from the back post. To actually have the fans, all 36,000 of them, cheering and singing your name – I know that it made my wife cry. It just shows you that it was a special time and I think that was the game where people remembered me for what I did. That game changed the opinion of a lot of people. I think that they saw another side of what I could do.

'I was never going to be a flamboyant player, I was never going to score your 25 goals, but what I would do was give 100 percent. And I wouldn't hide in a game. John Beresford said to me, "Sometimes you are your own worst enemy because you are too honest. If you are having a bad game, keep out of the way." But it wasn't in my nature to be like that. The Crystal Palace game in the FA Cup was one of those games where you do things, you're crossing balls with your left foot even though Ruud said I couldn't use my left foot. We ended up clawing our way through it in the third round and it was a good day. From there really, I had a very good time and obviously it was the game that got us on the road in the FA Cup.'

It seemed a real shame to bring Warren back down to earth, but my second youngest son made his debut as a Newcastle United supporter accompanying me to the FA Cup fourth round game at St James' Park on 26 January 1997. Newcastle hosted Nottingham Forest and lost 2–1. Unfortunately, a wayward header by Warren set one of the goals up, and my son demanded that I mention it. He was only seven at the time and, nine years on, he wanted an explanation.

'If you could have chalk and cheese, that was it. It was a game where, if I'm being honest to myself, for a little while I didn't play that badly. I made two horrendous mistakes, one horrendous mistake with a header, and then it went from bad to worse. And when you are having a nightmare, you just want someone to get you out of it. I mean, I'd had deflection off a shot. Ian Woan had a shot before and it took a deflection, but I think the header and everything else that evolved around it at the time with the way the team was playing, I put myself on a plate and it was a bad time for me.

'But it was about character. That was what playing non-League football gave to me. I wasn't going to walk away and hide. Probably at the time after that game, a lot of people would have loved me to walk away, but it wasn't in my nature. I knew what a special club this was and I didn't want to walk away. At the end of the day, you've got to walk away when the time is right, as it was with Bobby Robson, but at that time I didn't want to do that. They were tough times, they were hard times, but that's when you find out a lot about yourself and the people around you. And I managed to claw myself back into it.'

Warren had managed to get himself into the England squad and was selected to play his full debut in Dublin in 1995. It was to prove to be a rather disappointing and alarming experience that lasted less than half an hour.

'I'd been in the squad for about 18 months beforehand and I'd been around the set-up with Graham Taylor as well, so I had a little taste of it. Finally, I got my chance against the Republic of Ireland, which was a big game. There was a lot of hype about that game: it was a big game for me to be playing for England. It was a game that Terry [Venables] wanted to play me in. It didn't start as well as we had hoped, we were 1–0 down and then you get a load of mindless thugs and idiots wrecking the stand. The main concern for me at that time was that my wife and my family were in that part of the stadium. I wasn't actually sure where they were. It was a bit surreal at the time because you're looking at it and just thinking, "Okay, they're going to stop in a minute". Then it just got worse and worse and in the end they had to call the game off. So that was one debut that I won't forget. I managed to get a cap for it anyway. David Kelly, who was also at Newcastle, got their goal and he was credited with that. It was an upsetting time really. You build yourself up and you look forward to it, and those people don't realise what they've done to someone. At the end of the day, that was the bad part of society that you have to deal with.'

As a record defender Warren came up against some tough opponents and he recalled a few of them.

Chapter 12: WARREN BARTON

'People like Ryan Giggs, because if you play against Manchester United and you do well against Ryan Giggs, then they'd bring on Lee Sharpe at the time. But I never felt uncomfortable. I had to raise my game against them. When we played against Juventus with Zidane, it was only a friendly game in San Marino, but they were special players. Alan Shearer, when he played for Blackburn, was a strong player. Ian Wright at the time would be in your ear every two minutes and people like Harry Kewell. Dwight Yorke, when he played for Aston Villa, and I played for Wimbledon, he played on the left wing and he gave me a tough time. But there was never anyone I feared. Even when we played against David Ginola, when he was at Spurs, you knew what he could do to someone. But I think that made you lift your game. You knew that if you were going to get a good tackle in, the fans would like it as well. They were on your side as well, so you had that with you. Thierry Henry, if you're not on your game, he will tear you to pieces. In training I always used to try and mark Peter Beardsley, or Les Ferdinand, or Alan Shearer, because you wanted to put yourself up against the best. I was lucky enough to play against a lot of quality players. Luis Figo, when we played against Barcelona, playing against someone like that, it was another special occasion.'

Even when things were not going right for Warren on the pitch, he never gave up. As he said, his character saw him through and in the end he won over a lot of his critics. During his stay on Tyneside he enjoyed his relationship with the supporters.

'I had seven fantastic years there, I enjoyed it, even with the ups and the downs, but I never had a problem with the fans. You know, if you're walking round town and you're chatting to fans, if you've been okay, they'll be okay with you. It was quite funny, when I was at the Manchester United game, the fans were cheering for Robert, which I found strange. He allegedly criticised the club and the area and yet the fans forgave him for that. Some players decide that they won't do something and they get away with it. I think that's football fans in general. But when we've been out in town, we've never had a problem with the fans. The response when I left, I must have got 200–300 letters from fans. I think that because of what I did, I proved myself at the club, not only football-wise but also in the community. The people at the club, the guys who opened the doors for us, all the stewards, all the other people, I tried to help them feel a part of the football club. When they say that you're an adopted Geordie and you're a Londoner, you know that you've done okay. It's nice to be felt in high esteem by the fans.'

During his career with Newcastle United, Warren experienced working under four different managers.

'They were all different in their own way. I think that Bobby Robson was the best as a whole package, as a manager, as a man-manager and because of his commitment to the area. He knew what the club was all about. Kevin Keegan was great. When we were winning and things were going well, he was fantastic. Stopping off at McDonald's on the way home after beating Everton 3–1, all things like that, they were special times. And that's how he was when things were going well. Obviously we had the shock as a nation when he left. Kenny Dalglish to an extent was great for me because he brought me back into the set-up, at Middlesbrough away. We ended up winning the game 1–0. I was playing in a holding midfield role. As I said before, Ruud Gullit played me at left-back against Crystal Palace. I played a lot of games under Ruud.

'I've been very fortunate, touch wood, that I have got on with all the managers, particularly Bobby who made me vice-captain and then captain when Alan Shearer was injured. They were all unique in their own way and all had their own, not faults as such, but identities. With Kevin, when it wasn't going well, it was how do we change it, what do we do? With Kenny it was never the players' fault. He took too much responsibility. He should have said that we were crap at certain times and I think people would have respected him a lot more for that. Ruud was just Ruud in his own way.

Chapter 12: WARREN BARTON

Football-wise, he was excellent, but his man-management wasn't. You could see what happened at Chelsea and you could see what happened at Newcastle. You could see the sort of mentality that he had. But I think Bobby was the best as a package. Funnily enough, coming up on the train for the game yesterday, who was two seats in front of me? Sir Bobby. He came over and he chats to me for three and a half hours.'

Most Newcastle United players are honoured by the supporters with a chant or a song that fits their personality or skills on the ball. With Warren, it was his barnet. The song was 'Warren Barton, centre partin', tra la la la…'.

'I think when you come to a certain age, and you being a gentleman as you are will know that, you have to change with the times. The hairline and the image were alright when you're in your mid-20s, but when you get into your mid-30s/early 40s you've got to start changing it. I might grow it back again, you never know. I think I'm probably the only player to have a song after his hair, which is quite strange. Normally it's about your talent or about scoring goals, but mine was about my hair. I suppose one day I'll have to grow it back again. I do look at it sometimes and cringe. I might have a side parting. We'll see if they can make up a song about that.

'People ask me about Newcastle. I think if you ask any player in the Premier League, they would love to play for this club because of the fans, the people, the city and what it all stands for. Once you are here, you know that the fans are fantastic. The home fans are not always as good as the away fans, but they still make that noise.'

Prominent features of the modern games at St James' Park have been supporters booing and the early leavers. I asked Warren for his views on these.

'I remember playing at home against Bradford and against Watford, winning 1–0 at half-time, and getting booed off by the fans. I remember playing for Wimbledon against Newcastle and being 4–0 down within 20 minutes because people were coming at you from everywhere. The high tempo of the game was what the fans wanted. They'd worked hard all week and they expected you to go at the other team from that first whistle to the last whistle. It was our stadium, it was our pitch and we had to take the game to them. Teams would come to Newcastle and try to stifle the game, and try to make the crowd turn on their own players.

'People leaving early, maybe it's to beat the traffic, but they get stuck anyway. When they have paid their money and it's 0–0 and nothing's happening, they could probably justify reasons for leaving. But I don't understand why people pay such money and they leave before the end. At the end of the day you're in the entertainment business and if you're not pulling your weight, it does leave you open to criticism. What players have got to do is to take responsibility. They sometimes even hide away behind the manager's tactics. At the end of the day you go out and play football. They get paid a fortune to do that and they are there to perform. If they don't perform, they are there to be criticised.'

Warren moved on from Newcastle United in 2002, when he was transferred to Derby County. It was a move that was not without some sadness.

'It was difficult when I got left out by Bobby Robson, going from being vice-captain and captain to not actually making the squad. Bobby respected me and he turned round and said afterwards, "Look, I didn't want you just travelling and being a squad member. I felt too much for you, you had to leave, whether that's right or wrong." It was very difficult to leave, but now I know that it was the right time for me. I was 33, all but a few days, and he was looking to bring in other players. He did the same with Gary Speed and with Rob Lee. Once you get to that sort of age, you can't perform at that level every week. Being the players that we were, we wanted to play every week. So, we weren't happy to play one in four. Alan Shearer had a situation when he was being rested. You don't want to be rested, you want to be playing as often as you can. Bobby did say to me, "Look, stay here, we'll give you another year, then try and get into the coaching side of it." I said, "Gaffer, I want to play, I feel fit, and I feel like I want to play." He just said, "Well, when it's the right club, you make that decision."

'The opportunity was there to go to Derby. So yeah, it was difficult because I knew that anywhere from Newcastle was going downwards, and that's no disrespect to Derby or anyone else. But it would be a step down moving from Newcastle. At the time it was right for me to move. Looking back now, it was justified because I was 33 and I wanted to go on for another couple of years. That's what happened when I had the opportunity to go to Derby. I didn't want to stay at Newcastle and people say that I should've gone. I didn't want people saying that my legs had gone and I couldn't do it anymore. After all, they said that when I was 27. I decided that it was time for me to go and it was the same when I decided to retire as well.'

The mid-1990s on Tyneside will always be remembered for the Keegan era of the 'Entertainers' and there were some great moments on and off the pitch. Warren recalled the team punishment for getting things wrong.

'If you ever made a mistake, you had to do press-ups. It didn't matter if you had just fallen over or you were being interviewed, you had to do them. Kevin himself did it one time. He gave the ball away to the wrong person and he did his press-ups. I remember one really funny moment when I think we were at Selhurst Park. Peter Beardsley went to take a corner and he kicked the corner flag. It was supposed to be a serious game but he had to do his press-ups. That was quite a funny moment.'

Playing as a defender, Warren always needed to make certain that his tackles were timed right. Of course there was one famous occasion when his timing was a little off.

'I remember once at Newcastle, we were having our Christmas night out and on the way home, nature called. I was on my way home in a taxi – this could only happen in the North East – I got into a taxi and the driver was a Mackem, a Sunderland supporter. We had to go round the streets to get back up onto the central motorway and I said, "I'm not going to make it home, nature's calling, and I just need to go." He stopped the taxi in the middle of the road so that I could get out. It was just my luck that a police van comes along and pulls up beside him, and this officer asks, "What are you doing?" Instead of just saying that he had pulled over for some reason he said, "I'm waiting for him over there, Warren Barton." The police came over and I got a bit of a telling off. So, that was very embarrassing. I think the headline in the paper was "A wee the lads". It happens, but it could've been a lot worse.'

Warren is now a partner in a travel company based in the North East. By his own admission, when the company was set up he knew nothing about the business, but he had the contacts.

'People who I know get four or five weeks off in the summer and they like to cram everything in there. They want everything tailor-made, if you like, everything done for them. It's been getting on for six years now. We employ five local people up here and touch wood, it's been going well, considering we've had a terrorist attack and a war. We've done okay; we're doing alright. It's something that runs itself and I keep involved in as much as I can, but it runs itself to be honest with you.'

In the world of football, it is difficult for players to win over all the supporters all of the time. Even the greatest of players will have off days and will attract criticism. Warren was an honest player who accepted the views of his critics and always did his best to put things right on the pitch. There is no doubt, even now, that leaving Newcastle United was a sad occasion for Warren at the time, but he accepts that it was meant to be. You could say that it was a case of hair today, gone tomorrow.

Postscript

STOPPAGE TIME

AS THE FLOODLIGHTS begin to fade, the divots are put back and the crowd disperses to a variety of chosen watering holes once again, it is time to reflect upon another performance. The manager will be giving his post-match interviews, while the players are drying off after welcome showers and are no doubt nursing a fresh set of bruises. I guess that some things do not change all that much; it is only the comfort levels that change.

I have now interviewed many former players of Newcastle United Football Club and, although they achieved varying levels of success at St James' Park, they shared a common goal – to do their utmost for the club. Wearing the famous black and white shirt, every player contributed something significant and something unique to the history of Newcastle United.

There will always be 'Magpie Memories' as long as Newcastle United Football Club lives and breathes. As players retire or move on, there will be new blood, new players who will fill the void and proudly wear the famous shirt. All players who run out onto the hallowed turf at St James' Park in the future will ultimately build up a store of their own personal memories of games gone by – some good, some not so good and some occasionally outstanding.

There have been many changes in the world of football over the decades, as again highlighted during my interviews. Some of these changes were inevitably for the better; sadly some others were not. Former players, who played on pitches with very little grass, would relish the opportunity to perform on the modern-day surfaces. Centre-forwards from the 1950s and 1960s, who still bear the scars from heading the old laced leather footballs, can only dream of leaping for the modern ball as it is crossed into the penalty area.

Looking back and hearing stories of professional footballers staying in humble digs with landladies and using public transport to get to matches makes you realise just how fortunate the modern-day stars are. Young players today can afford to buy large houses and to drive around in super motorcars. Sadly the money available in football now has changed the very nature of the game.

All-seater stadiums, corporate hospitality and season-ticket allocations have all influenced the development of football today. Supporters have changed. Being passionate about the game and your team is no longer the only element required. To support your local team nowadays, you need to be able to find a lot of money. Of course, for some of the younger supporters of today, it is not a problem when their parents pay their pocket money by direct debit.

There is one significant element of the game of football that has not changed. In most genres, people become heroes and legends after they have knocked on Heaven's door. Fortunately for those who play the game, this is not the case with football. Players are given the opportunity to enjoy such cult status while they are still alive. Of course, some of these players maintain such elevated status long after they have disappeared off the radar.

Since the composition of football crowds has changed in recent years, the relationship between the players and the supporters has inevitably changed as well. Football supporters pay out a lot of money and demand a lot more in return. Whereas in the past players were usually given a chance to win the supporters over if they did not immediately perform well or were not instantly liked, the modern crowds seem to be far less tolerant and are perhaps far less forgiving.

Footballers today cannot hide anymore. Television saturation has ensured that every performance is analysed over and over again. Players can no longer pretend to be someone that they are not. I know exactly how it feels. Picture the scene. There I am walking the pedigree mongrel and I am being approached by a gorgeous young lady who is jogging towards me. I do what most men would do, stick out the chest, suck in the stomach flab and try to look fit. It is at that crucial moment that you realise in your hand you are carrying a see-through plastic bag full of fresh dog poo.

In many ways it is unfortunate that some players – those who fail to gain cult status – still contribute significantly to the overall development and history of a football club but they are not given the recognition that they perhaps richly deserve. I have personally been very fortunate to have talked to some of these players and there are many others who are perhaps still with us in spirit. In the immortal words of Lennon and McCartney, 'Some are dead and some are living, in my life I've loved them all.'

I have now written two books about Newcastle United Football Club, as seen through the eyes of former players, and I continue to live in the 'shadow' of St James' Park. It is quite interesting that when meeting with some of the players, they do not always seem to be the same as you would expect in 'real life'. Some are taller; some are smaller. Of course, they all fall within a certain height range. Let's be honest, if they were over seven feet tall, they would have played basketball, and if they were under five feet, I guess that they would likely have ridden horses. Then again, watching Newcastle United can often be like partaking in a rodeo. It can be exhilarating and sometimes it can be quite painful. I have seen some Newcastle United teams that looked great on paper.

Unfortunately, sometimes they were not all that great on grass. But that is football and that is the way it is with Newcastle United. Always expect the unexpected.

I have often been asked if I have a favourite from my collection of personal interviews with former Newcastle United players. I usually say, 'Oh yeah, that's easy, the next one.' I have thoroughly enjoyed all my interviews with the former players, but the anticipation of more stories and recollections will always make the next one that little bit special. For me it has been a privilege to spend time with former players who were willing to share memories of a significant part of their lives. As Albert Einstein once said, 'Only a life lived for others is a life worthwhile.'

I had hoped by the time this book was being put on the shelves of the bookshops on Tyneside that Newcastle United would have had a pristine trophy to parade round the streets of the city centre. Sadly, the trophy cabinet, like the frustrated supporters of the club, was yet again left feeling empty after a season of major disappointment. I am assuming that Newcastle United have a trophy cabinet rather than a room, since they don't win anything to justify having a room. Of course, notwithstanding the usual summer of discontent, season tickets will have been renewed and St James' Park will yet again look like barcode city.

Supporters of Newcastle United, young and not so young, have been brought up on a regular diet of disappointment for a long time now, mainly due to the annual aspirations of winning that elusive silverware.

However, we should not dismiss the fact that, starting with the second coming of Kevin Keegan, Newcastle United have experienced Premiership football since 1993 and have regularly ventured into Europe, giving supporters the opportunity to visit some wonderful destinations. There is little doubt that the bandwagon started rolling with Keegan in 1992 and without that change of fortune, Newcastle United were seriously at risk of following the same flight plan as Amelia Earhart. Indeed, things could have been a lot worse.

So, there you have it, the turnstiles have been locked, the floodlights have been switched off and the terraces have been swept ready for the next match. However, in the city of Newcastle upon Tyne, football fever will never diminish. Supporters will look ahead to the next game, whether it is at home or away, with great relish. That's how 'Magpie Memories' are born.

Acknowledgements

T he author wishes to extend his gratitude, which knows no bounds, to the following: Steve Caron (Chairman and Managing Director), Susan Last (Commissioning Editor), and all the team at Breedon Books Publishing; Allan Jacques, colleague and critic; Mark Jensen (Editor), for providing me with a vehicle for my early literary journey in 'The Mag'; Kinky Friedman, for making me his honorary Texas cousin and convincing me that you are never too o-l-d to start writing; my family, for all their support and understanding; the Newcastle Dog and Cat Shelter, for allowing the pedigree mongrel dog to share my settee; and last but not least, all those who have played for Newcastle United Football Club, without whom this series would never have been possible.

'Newcastle as a football club, Newcastle as a city, and Newcastle fans are the best and deserve the best.'

Kevin Keegan (1993)

'One of the hardest things about being a writer is selecting a genre and then remembering to use the word "genre" as often as possible in your interviews.'

Kinky Friedman (2002)